creating

CooL KiD STuFF

CREATIVE
PUBLISHING
international

MINNETONKA, MINNESOTA

10311728

President/CEO: David D. Murphy

CREATING COOL KID STUFF
Created by: The Editors of Creative Publishing international

Executive Editor: Elaine Perry
Managing Editor: Yen Le
Senior Editor: Linda Neubauer
Senior Art Director: Stephanie Michaud
Desktop Publishing Specialist: Laurie Kristensen
Project & Prop Stylist: Joanne Wawra
Samplemakers: Arlene Dohrman, Teresa Henn
Photo Stylists: Arlene Dohrman, Joanie Michaud,
   Joanne Wawra
Studio Services Manager: Marcia Chambers
Photographers: Tate Carlson, Andrea Rugg
Director of Production Services: Kim Gerber
Contributor: Walnut Hollow

Special thanks to the following for the use of their homes:
   Patricia and Dave Murphy; Linda and Gary Neubauer;
   Aimee and Greg Spivak

ISBN 1-58923-015-9

Printed on American paper by:
Quebecor World
10 9 8 7 6 5 4 3 2 1

Creative Publishing international, Inc. offers a variety of how-to books.
For information write:
   Creative Publishing international, Inc.
      Subscriber Books
   5900 Green Oak Drive
   Minnetonka, MN 55343

Due to differing conditions, materials, and skill levels, the publisher and
various manufacturers disclaim any liability for unsatisfactory results or
injury due to improper use of tools, materials, or information in this
publication.

Library of Congress Cataloging-in-Publication Data

Creating cool kid stuff.
   p. cm.
   Includes index.
   ISBN 1-58923-015-9 (pbk.)
   1. Handicraft. 2. Children's paraphernalia.   I. Creative Publishing International.

TT157 .C714 2001
745.5--dc21
                        2001042305

CONTENTS

Creative Playthings

Cuddly cute stuff

Delightful ideas

Personal touches

Introduction

Toy stores are packed to the rafters with the latest games and gizmos for kids. As parents, we can spend a small fortune trying to ensure that our kids stay busy and have fun. *Creating Cool Kid Stuff* gives us the opportunity to have a little creative fun of our own, making toys, games, and other cool stuff for our lucky kids. Every project in this book began as a bright idea from one of our staff members. We had a blast designing and creating these items and testing them out on our own kids.

In searching for "cool" ideas, our first objective was to make things that kids would think were "cool." After all, no matter how unique an item is or how much fun we had making it, if it doesn't catch a kid's attention, it's worthless. Secondly, a project may be similar to something that is available in a store, but there are advantages to making the item: it is far less expensive, the item can be made sturdier or better in some way, or it can be made with a few more bells and whistles. We also believe there is still value in the personal satisfaction gained from making special things for our kids.

With each project, you will find a complete shopping list of materials, as well as a list of the necessary tools. We have used common, inexpensive materials like PVC pipe, craft foam, vinyl sheeting, and polyurethane foam as the main requirements for many of our creations. Some items take advantage of useful products like chalkboard paint, polystyrene pellets, magnets, or specialty fabrics. All of the materials necessary to complete the projects are available at department stores, fabric and craft stores, or home improvement centers. Some items require sewing skills and a sewing machine; others require common household tools and basic carpentry skills. For a few projects, you'll need only simple crafting skills and a paintbrush or scissors.

For every project that needs them, complete patterns are given; some are full-size, others need to be enlarged on a copy machine or hand-drawn grid. As an added bonus, we've given you an indication of kids' appropriate ages for each project, the approximate cost of the materials, and the time it may take to complete the basic project. Of course, the more bells and whistles you add to the basic project, the higher the cost and the more time it will take to complete. You can plan accordingly.

Safety is an important feature to consider, no matter what the age of the kids. If the kids are around while you are creating this cool stuff, be sure sharp tools and cans of spray paint or other toxic products are out of reach. When used properly and by kids of the right ages, these finished items are safe. Parental assistance is sometimes necessary for setting up or moving some of the larger items.

When the word gets around that you've made all these fabulous things for your kids, your house will probably become the favorite neighborhood play center. Delightful giggles and enthusiastic thank-you hugs will be your reward. Our goal will be met if you also enjoy the process of creating cool kid stuff.

Yours truly,

The Cool Kid
Stuff Staff

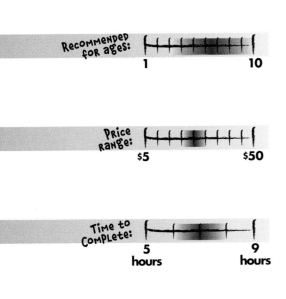

Recommended for ages:
1   10

Price range:
$5 $50

Time to complete:
5 hours   9 hours

LEAPIN' FROGS

Lily pads and beanbag frogs are the ingredients for this loads-of-fun versatile game. The ten numbered, skid-resistant, foam lily pads can be arranged any way imaginable to play hopscotch, musical chairs, or target toss. Cute fabric frogs, in a variety of colors, are stuffed with beans to make them just the right weight for tossing with accuracy. The entire set stacks to a compact size for storing away in its own easy-to-sew tote.

Materials:

For lily pads:

Ten sheets of green craft foam, 12" × 18" (30.5 × 46 cm), 3 mm thick

Two sheets of black craft foam, 12" × 18" (30.5 × 46 cm), 2 mm thick

Four sheets of double-sided adhesive, 9" × 12" (23 × 30.5 cm), such as Double Tack™ by Grafix®

Graphite paper

¼ yd. (0.25 m) nonslip latex rug backing, 45" (115 cm) wide

Light green acrylic paint

For frogs:

Closely woven or knit fabric, two 6½" (16.3 cm) squares per frog

Thread

Small dry beans or rice, about ½ cup (125 mL) per frog

Two ¼" (6 mm) movable eyes per frog

Craft glue

For tote:

⅝ yd. (0.6 m) mediumweight frog-print fabric

Thread

14" (35.5 cm) zipper

Basting tape or glue stick

Transparent tape, ½" (1.3 cm) wide

18" (46 cm) nylon strap, 1" (2.5 cm) wide

Tools:

Copy machine

Craft knife and cutting board

Craft scissors; fabric scissors

Small paintbrush or foam applicator

Straightedge

Sewing machine; zipper foot

Iron

Point turner, optional

Funnel

Hand needle

Take-along fun   Multipurpose   Self-storing tote

1 Enlarge the half-size pattern on page 11, using a copy machine. Make one pattern of the lily pad outline and another of the leaf marking.

2 Trace and cut ten lily pads from green foam, using a craft knife and cutting board or craft scissors. Place leaf marking pattern on lily pad; trace. Paint marking with light green acrylic paint. Allow to dry, and repeat as necessary.

3 Draw five 1½" × 12" (3.8 × 30.5 cm) rectangles on the paper backing of a sheet of double-sided adhesive. Draw a line dividing all rectangles into two strips, 7" and 5" (18 × 12.7 cm) long. Repeat on a second sheet. Remove paper backing from opposite side and apply adhesive to rug backing.

4 Cut out strips, following marked lines. Remove paper backing and apply one long strip across the back of each lily pad. Cut smaller strips in half and apply each half to opposite sides of long strip.

5 Trace the mirror image number patterns (pages 12 and 13) onto two sheets of double-sided adhesive, using graphite paper. Remove paper backing from opposite side and adhere to black foam.

6 Cut out numbers. Remove paper backing and adhere numbers to centers of lily pads.

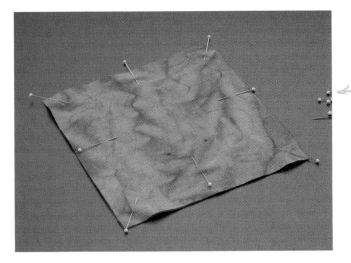

1 Cut two 6½" (16.3 cm) squares of fabric. Trace frog pattern onto wrong side of one square. Transfer small dots. Pin fabrics right sides together.

2 Stitch on marked line, using short stitches. Back-stitch at dots, leaving opening between dots.

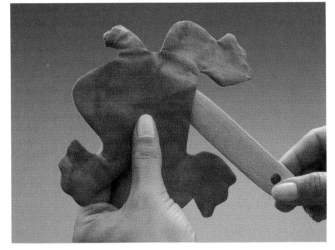

3 Stitch second row of stitches just outside first row. Trim excess fabric to within ⅛" (3 mm) of outer stitching line; trim to within ⅜" (1 cm) of marked line at opening. Clip corners and points close to first row of stitching.

4 Turn frog right side out through opening. Push out points and smooth seamline, using point turner or eraser end of a pencil.

5 Fill frog loosely with beans or rice. Slipstitch opening closed, using short stitches. Glue eyes in place.

Note: If you are concerned about the possibility of small children biting off the eyes and choking, omit the eyes, embroider them, or paint them on with craft paint. Or apply safety eyes before stitching the layers together.

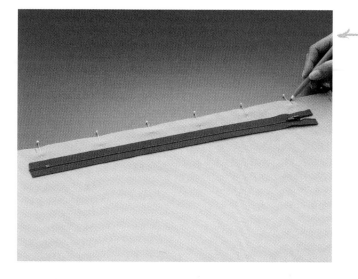

1 Cut two pieces of fabric 20" (51 cm) square. Pin the fabric, right sides together, along one side on the lengthwise grain. Center the zipper alongside the edges, and mark the seam allowances just above and below the zipper stops.

2 Stitch a ½" (1.3 cm) seam from the edge to the first mark, backstitching at the beginning and end. Repeat at the opposite end. Machine baste between the marks. Finish the raw edges on all four sides of both fabric pieces. Press the seam allowances open.

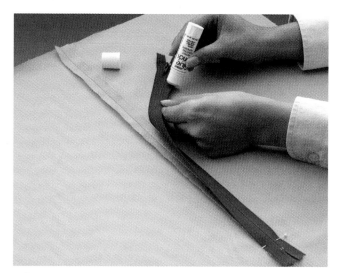

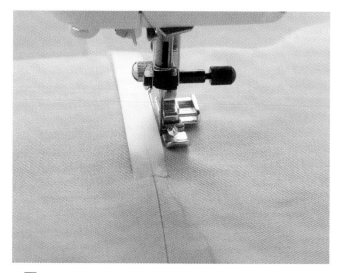

3 Apply basting tape or glue stick to the right side of the zipper tape along outer edges. Place the zipper face-down over the basted part of the seam.

4 Spread tote pieces flat, right side up. Center a strip of ½" (1.3 cm) transparent tape over the seamline, between zipper stops. Stitch along outer edges of tape and across ends, using zipper foot. Remove tape. Remove basting stitches.

5 Open zipper. Pin tote pieces, right sides together, along remaining three sides. Stitch ½" (1.3 cm) seam.

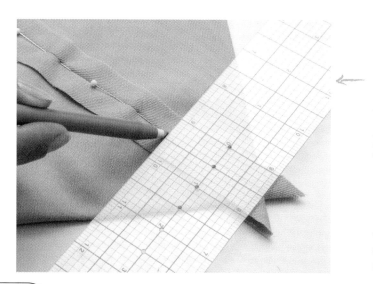

6 Separate pieces at one corner. Center seams on each side of corner, pinning through seams to make sure they are aligned. Mark a point on seamline, 2" (5 cm) from corner. Draw a line through mark perpendicular to seam, from fold to fold. Repeat at each corner.

7 Stitch on marked line for corners opposite the zipper. For corners next to the zipper, insert ends of strap into corner before stitching; trim strap corners as necessary. Stitch a second time to secure. Turn tote right side out and insert lily pads and frogs.

Patterns for Leapin' Frogs Game

Hint: Stabilize the tote bottom with a 2" × 16" (5 × 40.5 cm) strip of wood or foam-core board. Glue fabric to the strip and secure it to the tote bottom corners with self-adhesive Velcro®.

Enlarge lily pad 200%

Numbers for Leapin' Frogs Game

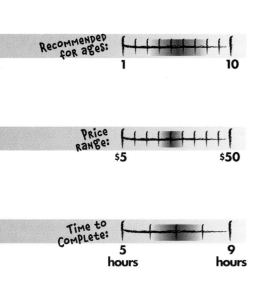

Recommended for ages:
1   **10**

Price range:
$5   **$50**

Time to Complete:
5 hours   **9 hours**

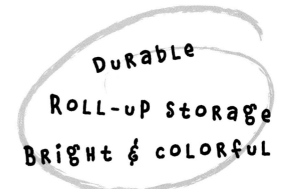

INDOOR HOPSCOTCH

Kids don't have to wait for a sunny day to play hopscotch. This bright, cheerful, garden path hopscotch board is ready to roll out indoors, no matter what the weather. Made of durable, polyester outdoor canvas, the game board is easy to make and just as easy to store away. Quick-sew bean bugs are perfect for tossing and marking one's place.

The canvas is manufactured 32" (81.5 cm) wide, just the right width for the hopscotch board. The neat, stable selvages provide finished sides, and the cut ends do not ravel—no sewing is necessary.

The design is stenciled onto the fabric with opaque acrylic paints, using stencils you cut yourself. Numbers for the stepping stones are masked out, using self-adhesive vinyl.

Materials:

- 2½ yd. (2.3 m) polyester outdoor canvas
- Opaque acrylic paints, in desired colors
- Paint pens
- Self-adhesive vinyl, such as Con-Tact®
- Stencil plastic
- Precut stencils of flowers and bugs, optional
- Repositionable stencil adhesive
- Tightly woven red fabric, two 4" (10 cm) squares per bean bug
- Black fabric marker or permanent marker
- Small dry beans or rice, about ⅓ cup (75 mL) per bean bug

Tools:

- Scissors
- Craft knife and cutting board or stencil-cutting iron
- Sponge roller; sponge pouncers; paper plate
- Pinking shears or pinking rotary cutter
- Sewing machine; zipper foot

Durable
Roll-up Storage
Bright & colorful

1 Cut canvas for the hopscotch board 90" (229 cm) long, making sure ends are perfectly square. Lightly mark guidelines for the stepping stones, following the photograph on page 14 or using your own design.

2 Trace the mirror image numbers on pages 18 and 19 onto the paper backing of self-adhesive vinyl; cut out numbers. Affix number masks to fabric in the center of each stepping stone.

3 Draw an irregular 11" (28 cm) circle on a sheet of stencil plastic, for stepping stone stencil. Cut out stencil, using craft knife and cutting surface, or stencil-cutting iron. Spray the back of the cutting stone stencil with repositionable stencil adhesive, following the manufacturer's directions.

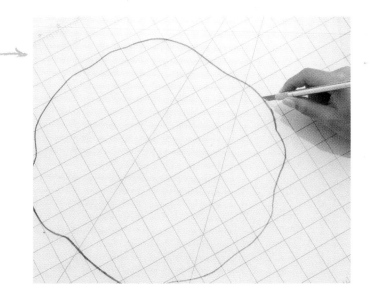

Hint: When cutting a stencil with a craft knife, draw the knife toward you, always keeping the knife tip on the cutting surface. Stop cutting with the knife tip in place and turn the stencil occasionally to improve your position.

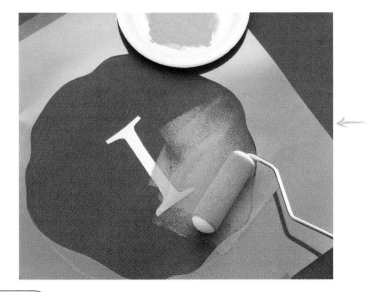

4 Position the stencil over a stepping stone, centering the number. Pour a puddle of paint onto a paper plate; roll the sponge roller through the paint, loading the roller evenly. Roll the paint over the stencil; reload roller as necessary. Remove the stencil.

5 Repeat step 4 for all the stepping stones, working in random locations to avoid wet paint. Allow to dry thoroughly. Remove the number masks.

6 Make stencils for the bugs and flowers, using the patterns on page 20. Or purchase precut stencils of bugs and flowers. Stencil the bugs and flowers using sponge pouncers. Paint details, using paint pens. Allow to dry thoroughly.

How to Make a Bean Bug

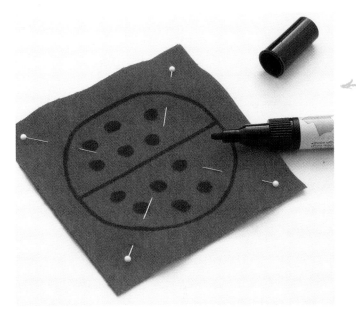

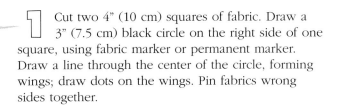

1 Cut two 4" (10 cm) squares of fabric. Draw a 3" (7.5 cm) black circle on the right side of one square, using fabric marker or permanent marker. Draw a line through the center of the circle, forming wings; draw dots on the wings. Pin fabrics wrong sides together.

2 Stitch on the outer edge of the circle, using short stitches. Backstitch, leaving a 1" (2.5 cm) opening.

3 Cut out bean bug ½" (1.3 cm) from stitching line, using pinking shears or a pinking rotary cutter. Fill bug loosely with rice or dry beans. Stitch the opening closed. Stitch second row of stitches just outside first row, using a zipper foot.

Numbers for Hopscotch

Patterns for Hopscotch Stencils

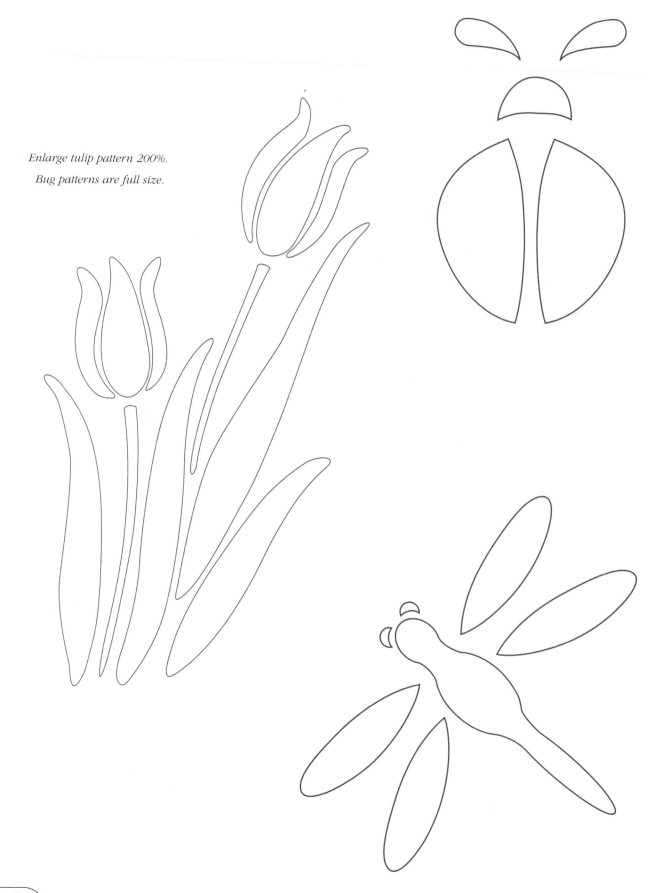

Enlarge tulip pattern 200%.

Bug patterns are full size.

Instead of tiptoeing through tulips, kids can play hopscotch in outer space. Design this game using outdoor canvas in a dark blue color. For each place marker, cut mirror image spaceships from adhesive-back craft foam or felt, and sandwich a metal washer between the layers.

Recommended for ages: |—|—|—|—|—|—|—|—|—|
1   10

Price range: |—|—|—|—|—|—|—|—|—|
$5 $50

Time to Complete: |—|—|—|—|—|
1   5
hour   hours

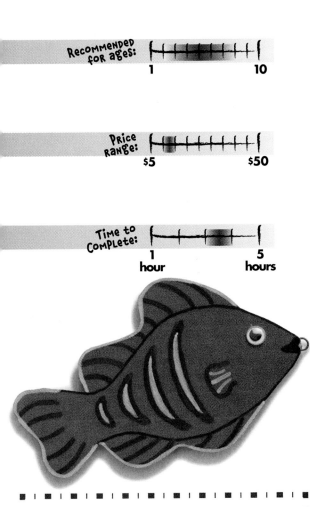

It takes a splash of patience, a drop of coordination, and a stringer-full of fun to reel in these fish. The magnet "hook" of the fishing pole attracts the metal paper clips, sandwiched securely between two layers of craft foam at the fish's mouth. The game can be played in the bathtub, in a backyard wading pool, or on the floor. Kids can go fishin' at birthday parties, when friends come to visit, or whenever they're in a fishin' frame of mind. Numbers can be painted on one side of the fish to add a squirt of competition for slightly older kids who want to keep score.

BUiLDS COORDiNATiON
Wet OR DRY
MaJOR fuN - MiNOR COST

Materials:

- Wooden dowel, ½" (1.3 cm) diameter, 24" (61 cm) long
- 1" (2.5 cm) ball knob
- Small wooden finial
- Two connecting screws; wood glue
- Horseshoe magnet, about 1" (2.5 cm) wide
- ¾ yd. (0.7 m) heavy cord
- Craft foam sheets in various colors, 2 mm thick
- Graphite paper
- Glue stick
- Colored metal paper clips
- Waterproof glue, such as Fabri-Tac™ or hot glue
- Paint pens; craft paints; decorations as desired

Tools:

- Drill; drill bit slightly smaller than connecting screws
- Small paintbrush
- Hot glue gun, optional
- Scissors, or craft knife and cutting board

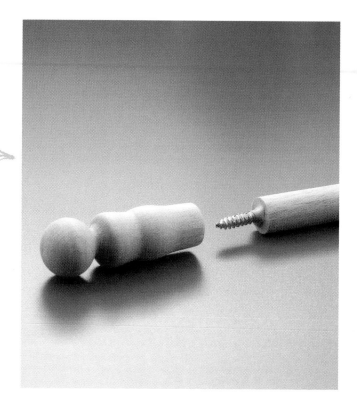

1. Drill a small hole in each end of the dowel; insert one end of a connecting screw in each hole. For handle, apply wood glue to the dowel end; attach finial to connecting screw, securing pieces snugly together. Wipe away excess glue.

Note: Select a small finial that is comfortable for a child to hold; a variety of styles will work. This one is actually a small wooden doll shape found in a craft store.

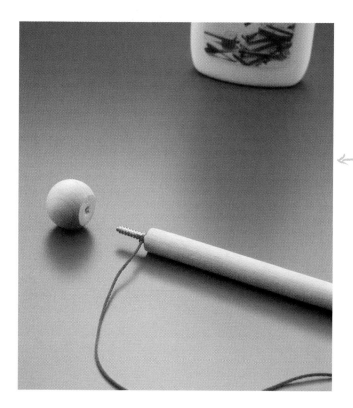

2. Tie small loop in end of cord. Apply wood glue to other dowel end, slip loop over connecting screw. Attach ball knob to connecting screw, screwing pieces snugly together. Wipe away excess glue.

3. Paint pole as desired. Tie magnet to end of cord. Secure with hot glue.

Hint: While we've eliminated sharp points as a safety issue with this game, a chunky magnet flying at the end of a string can raise a welt. Encourage still fishing as opposed to casting!

4 Transfer fish and turtle patterns (pages 26 and 27) to sheet foam, using graphite paper. Secure two pieces of foam together temporarily with glue stick. Cut out figures, using scissors, or craft knife and cutting board, cutting through both layers.

5 Separate figure halves. Decorate figures as desired, using paint pens or acrylic paints; allow to dry thoroughly.

6 Open one bend of paper clip; place lengthwise on wrong side of one figure half, with small loop protruding at mouth. Glue halves together securely, using waterproof glue. Weight figures until glue is set.

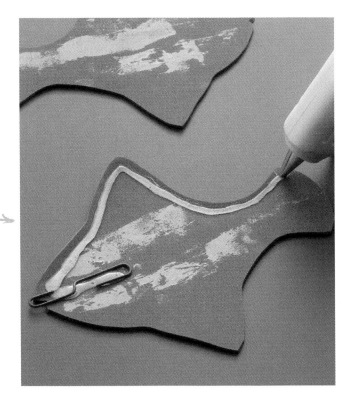

Recommended for ages:

1   10

Price range:

$5 $50

Time to complete:

1   5
hour   hours

Materials for Basic Busy Box:

- Unfinished wooden box with sliding lid
- Primer for wood
- Satin latex paint or glossy acrylic paint
- Paint pens, foam rubber stamps, stencils as desired

Additional materials for travel box:

- Adhesive-backed craft foam
- Clear plastic sheet

Additional materials for pegboard box:

- Graph paper
- Golf tees; colored rubber bands; chalk

Tools:

Fine-grit sandpaper; tack cloth

Paintbrush

Craft knife and cutting surface for travel box

Drill and ³/₁₆" drill bit for pegboard box

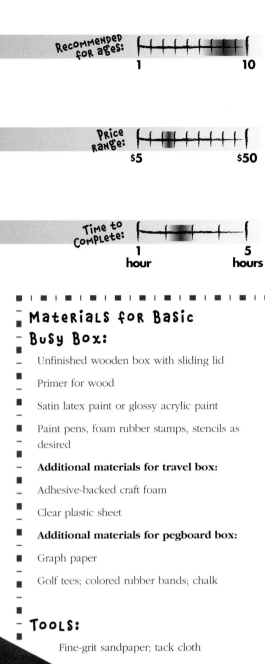

Busy Boxes

Unfinished wooden boxes with sliding lids are available in craft centers. Some have plain lids that can be painted to coordinate with the rest of the box. Another style comes with a chalkboard lid. They are a great beginning for personalized busy boxes that can be designed to suit the particular interests of any child. For instance, a travel box provides a way for a child to keep souvenirs and postcards from a family vacation or road trip; a frame on the cover holds postcards that can be changed as the trip progresses. A variety of games and activities can be played with a pegboard box, made from a blank box with a chalkboard lid.

To keep the box and lid from warping when they are painted, both sides of all surfaces should be primed and then painted. A satin finish latex or glossy acrylic paint will give the box a smooth finish that is easy to keep clean.

Encourages creativity

Personal

Portable

How to Make a Busy Box

1 Sand all surfaces smooth, using fine-grit sandpaper; wipe clean with tack cloth. For box with chalkboard lid, do not sand lid.

2 Apply wood primer to all surfaces; allow to dry. Sand lightly, if necessary. Paint surfaces with basecoat of satin latex paint or glossy acrylic paint. Avoid painting cover-slide slots. Allow to dry.

3 Decorate outside of box as desired, using foam rubber stamps, stencils, or hand-painted designs. Personalize boxes, using fine-tip paint pens. Or, to use the acrylic paints you have on hand, purchase Tip-Pen™ caps, made by Plaid®, to use in place of the regular caps on the paint bottles.

How to Make a Travel Box

Note: This frame will hold a 4" × 6" (10 × 15 cm) postcard or photograph.

1 Follow steps 1 to 3 for the basic box. Cut a rectangle of adhesive-backed craft foam 7½" × 5¾" (19.3 × 14.5 cm) for the postcard frame; cut out the opening 1" (2.5 cm) from all sides, using a craft knife and cutting surface. Cut two foam spacers for the sides 7½" × ½" (19.3 × 1.3 cm) and one spacer for the end 4¾" × ½" (12 × 1.3 cm). Cut a clear plastic rectangle 7" × 4¾" (18 × 12 cm).

2 Remove the paper backing from the frame. Adhere the spacer strips to the sides and one end, aligning the outer edges. Adhere the clear plastic, aligning one edge to the open end of the frame and abutting the spacers on the remaining sides.

3 Mark the placement of the frame on the center of the box lid. Remove the paper backing from the spacers. Adhere the frame to the cover. Decorate as desired.

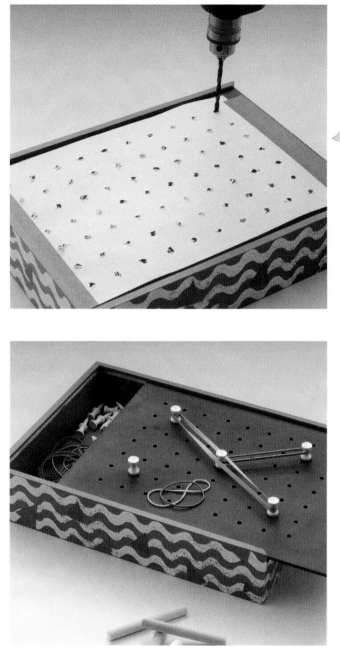

1 Follow steps 1 to 3 for the basic box, but do not paint chalkboard lid. Slide the lid in place. Tape graph paper to the lid. Drill ³⁄₁₆" holes in a 1" (2.5 cm) grid through lid. Fill the box with golf tees, colored rubber bands, and chalk.

Hint: If you are unable to find an unpainted box with a chalkboard lid, you can cut ⅛" (3 mm) MDF board to make a new lid. (The plain unpainted lids tend to splinter on the back side when drilling holes.) Drill the holes in the new lid before applying the chalkboard paint.

2a The golf tees can be put into the holes in many different combinations and connected with rubber bands to create geometric designs. A variety of games can also be played with this box: Kids can take turns connecting holes with vertical or horizontal chalk lines. When a player draws the last side of a square with his line, he puts his initial in the square. When the entire grid is filled, the winner is the one who claims the most squares.

2b Two kids can play a game of peg jumping: Fill all the holes but one with pegs. Take turns jumping a peg with another or moving a peg one hole vertically or horizontally. Jump as many pegs as you can with one move, removing pegs when they are jumped. When only one peg remains, the winner is the one with the most pegs.

Busy Boxes for Busy Kids

Design a box to thrill your amateur magician. Cover the outside of the box with glow-in-the-dark stickers or designs painted with glow-in-the-dark paint. Fill the box with magic tricks.

Encourage your kids to write letters to friends, relatives, or pen pals with a personal stationery box. Include blank note cards and envelopes, pens or pencils, rubber stamps and stamp pads, an address book, and a book of postage stamps. Mount small photocopied pictures of friends and family onto stamp-size rectangles of colored paper that you have cut with decorative-blade scissors to resemble postage stamps. Create a larger one using a picture of the child who will use the box. Decoupage the personal "stamps" onto the outside of the box, placing the owner's picture on the lid.

Recommended for ages:
1   10

Price Range:
$5 $50

Time to Complete:
1 hour   5 hours

MATERIALS:

- Fabric for body and face of puppet; knits preferred for face
- Fabric scraps for ears, eyes, and noses as desired
- Embroidery floss, buttons, or safety eyes and noses as desired
- Fabric glue
- Polyester fiberfill
- Thread
- Pompoms, heavy thread, chenille stems, yarn, felt for additional features

TOOLS:

- Fabric scissors
- Pins
- Iron
- Sewing machine
- Hand needle

INSPIRES imagination
CHILD-size fit

PUPPETS

Hand puppets are marvelous play tools for storytelling and fantasy building. Their role in fostering creative thinking and imagination is boundless. Kids also love to get involved in designing and creating their own puppets. Two basic patterns, one for animals and one for people, are used to create all of the puppets shown here, with variations developed by applying different facial features, ears, fur, or hair. Plush fabrics give animal puppets an authentic look; polyester fleece, robe velour, and synthetic knit suede are some options. Fabric scraps from your stockpile may be suitable for ear linings or other features, or great finds could be waiting in the remnant bins at your favorite store. Simple costumes and props, like capes, crowns, aprons, bow ties, glasses, or shoulder bags give the puppets more versatility.

These puppets are so quick and easy to make, you can create a full cast of characters in no time. All seams are ¼" (6 mm) and are included in the pattern pieces. The puppets are sized to fit kids' hands; thumbs and fingers operate the puppet arms while two fingers fit snugly behind the padded face.

1 Trace and cut out the patterns on pages 39 to 43. Cut out the puppet pieces following the grainlines indicated on the patterns. Transfer any markings to the wrong side of the fabric for each piece.

2 Stitch the darts in the face. Apply facial features by hand embroidery, fabric pens, sewing on buttons, gluing felt, or securing safety eyes. See suggestions for whiskers, snouts, and teeth on page 38.

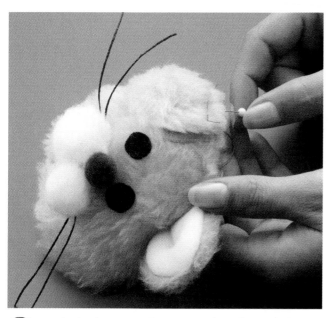

3 Stitch the lining to the ears, right sides together, leaving the bottom edge open. Turn right side out. Baste a small tuck in the center of the open edges. Baste ears to the right side of the face, lining side down, at the marks.

4 Stitch the face to the body front at the neck, right sides together. Press seam toward face. Turn under the bottom edge of the baffle ¼" (6 mm). Pin the baffle, right side up, to the wrong side of the face. Stitch, leaving the bottom edge open.

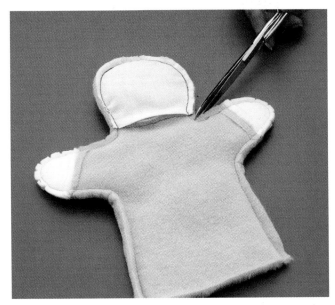

5 Stitch the hands to the front arms, right sides together; press seam allowances open. For people puppets, stitch hand backs and head back to body back. Pin the front to the back, right sides together. Stitch, easing back to fit front. Trim seam; notch outer curves, clip inner curves close to stitching line. Serge or zigzag the seam on woven fabrics.

6 Stuff face with polyester fiberfill. Slipstitch lower edge of baffle to seam allowance at neck. Turn puppet right side out.

Hint: Make a cast of puppets quicker by completing each step for several puppets at a time. Cut out and mark all the pieces in one work session, and store them in separate plastic bags.

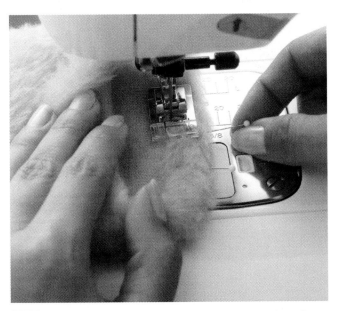

7 Turn under ½" (1.3 cm) hem at lower edge; for woven fabrics turn under ¼" (6 mm) double-fold hem. Stitch. Glue on or hand-stitch any additional trims.

Whiskers: Soak black carpet thread in craft glue or fabric stiffener; allow to dry. Thread a long needle to the center; knot ends together the desired whisker length from the end. Insert needle into one side of cheek area; bring out on opposite side. Tie knot close to exit hole; cut thread the desired whisker length. Repeat to make as many whiskers as desired.

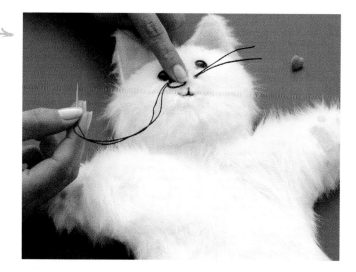

Snouts: Glue two 1" (2.5 cm) pompoms or one 1½" (3.8 cm) pompom to center of face, placing them over whisker knots, if the puppet has whiskers. Glue a ½" (1.3 cm) pompom above and between them for a nose or attach a heart-shaped button. Glue white felt teeth to face before applying whiskers and snout, if desired.

Manes: Wrap yarn closely around a strip of card stock or tear-away stabilizer cut twice as wide as the desired length of the mane. Place the wrapped strip over a strip of felt the same color as the mane. Stitch down the center with a short straight stitch. Tear away the card stock. Trim the felt as desired. Leave the mane looped or cut the loops. Glue the mane to the puppet.

People Hair: Cut a 3" × 4" (7.5 × 10 cm) scrap of felt in the same color as the hair. Place yarn strands side by side in the short direction, extending off the felt for bangs or nape hair. Stitch in place along front and back edges. Place yarn strands side by side in the long direction, over the first layer, extending off the felt about 6" (15 cm) on each side for braids or shorter for short hair. Stitch in center and at both edges. Make braids, if desired. Trim felt; glue to head.

Tails: Cut fabric strip 2" × 8" (5 × 20.5 cm). Fold strip right sides together over narrow cording, cut twice as long as the tail. Stitch across the end and ¼" (6 mm) from the long edges, using a zipper foot. Pull on the cord to turn the tail right side out. Cut off cord. Hand-stitch fringe or looped yarn to the tail end, if desired. To shape the tail, make small loops in the ends of a chenille stem; insert into tail before attaching to puppet body.

Puppet Patterns

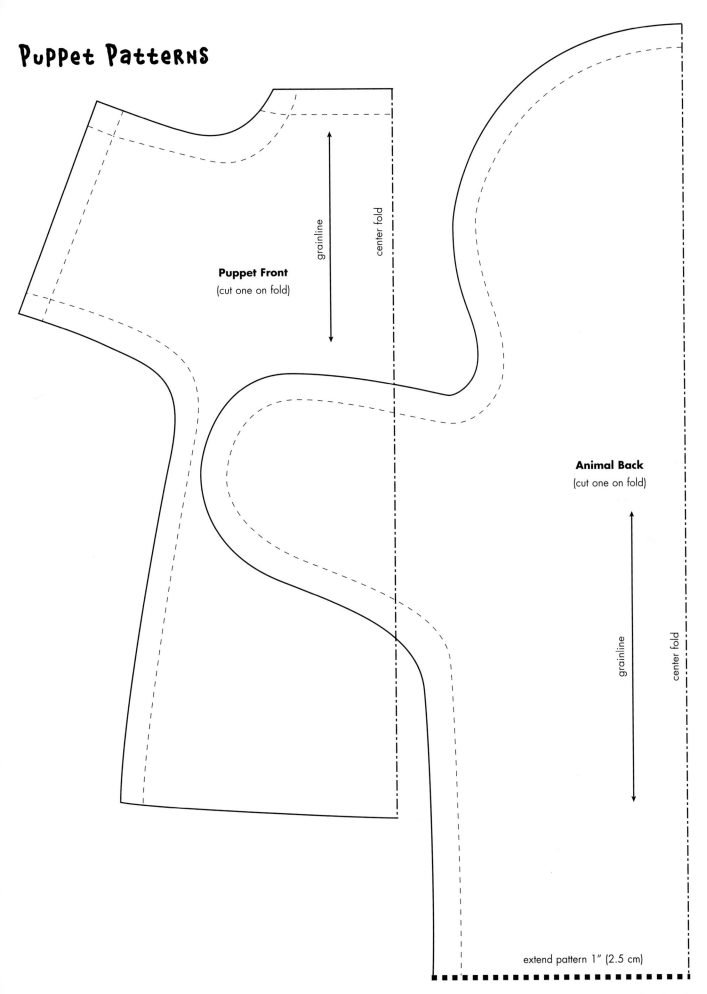

Puppet Front
(cut one on fold)

grainline

center fold

Animal Back
(cut one on fold)

grainline

center fold

extend pattern 1" (2.5 cm)

(continued)

Puppet Patterns
(continued)

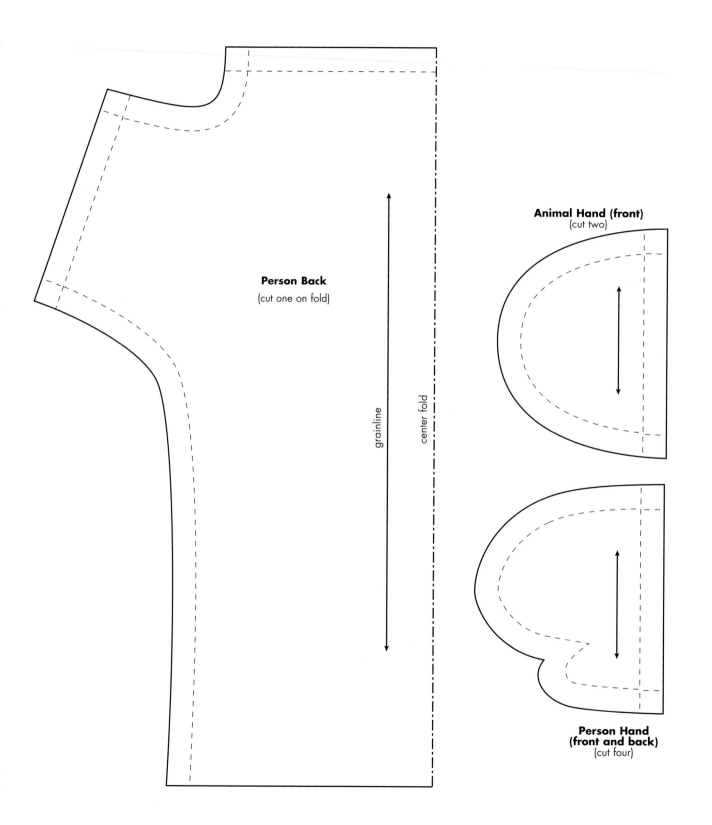

Person Back

(cut one on fold)

grainline

center fold

Animal Hand (front)
(cut two)

**Person Hand
(front and back)**
(cut four)

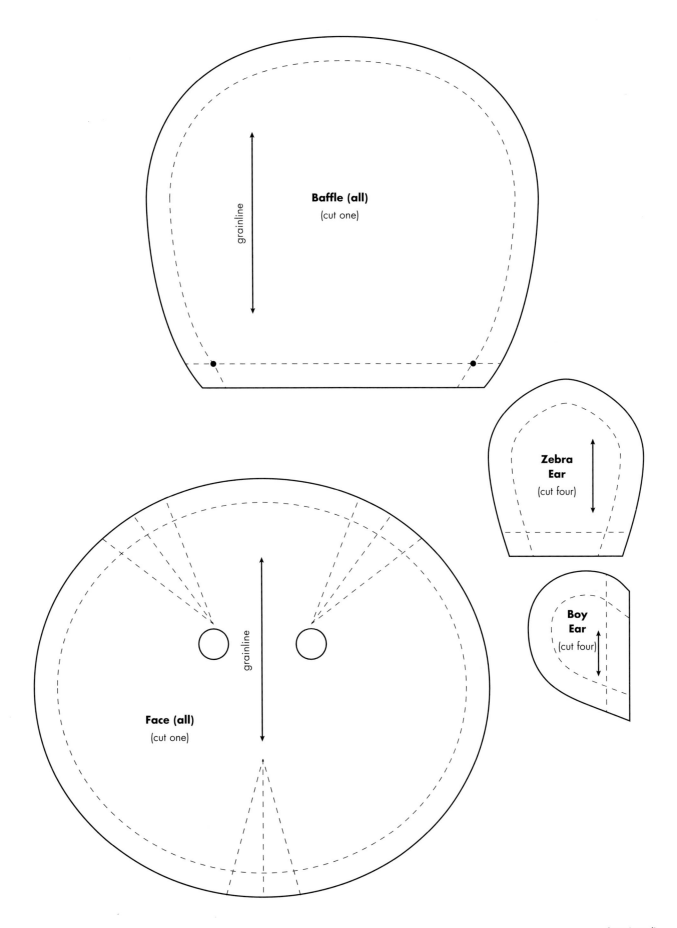

Baffle (all)
(cut one)

grainline

Zebra Ear
(cut four)

Face (all)
(cut one)

grainline

Boy Ear
(cut four)

(continued)

Puppet Patterns

(CONTINUED)

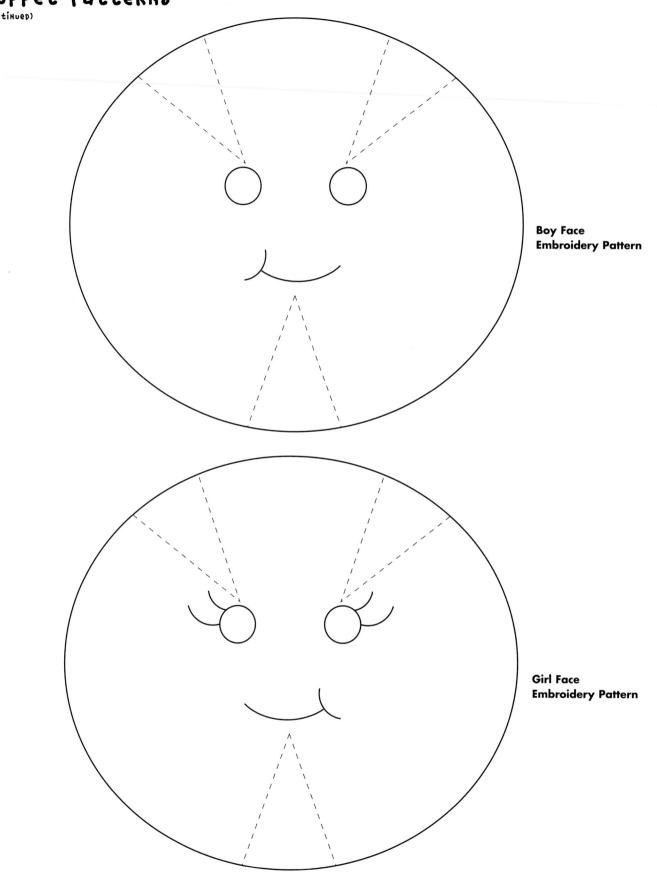

**Boy Face
Embroidery Pattern**

**Girl Face
Embroidery Pattern**

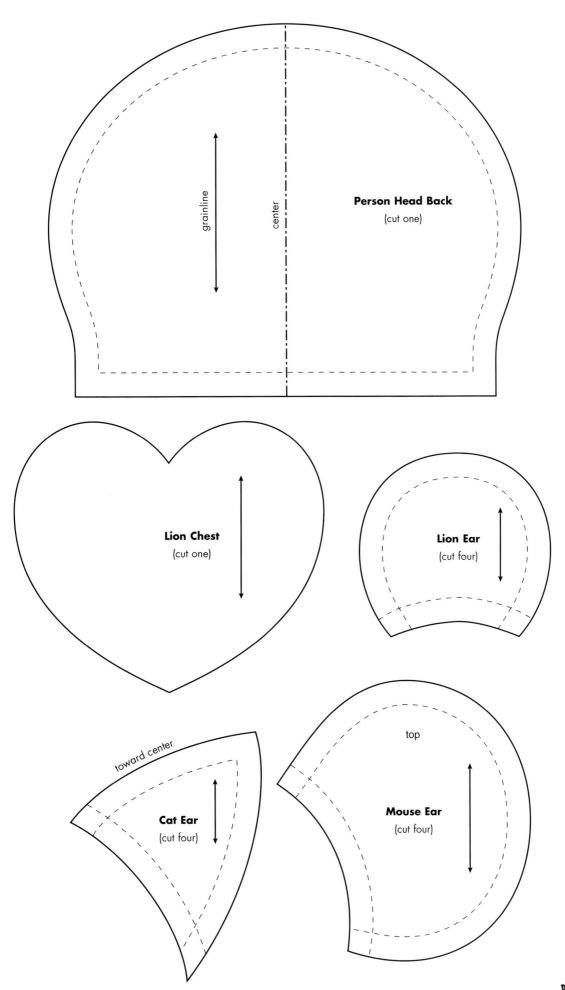

Person Head Back
(cut one)

grainline

center

Lion Chest
(cut one)

Lion Ear
(cut four)

toward center

Cat Ear
(cut four)

top

Mouse Ear
(cut four)

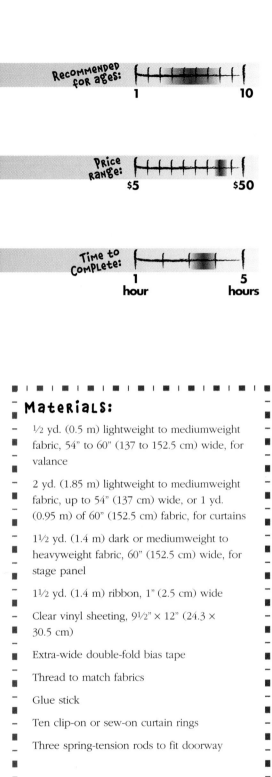

Recommended for ages:
1   10

Price Range:
$5 $50

Time to Complete:
1 hour   5 hours

Materials:

- ½ yd. (0.5 m) lightweight to mediumweight fabric, 54" to 60" (137 to 152.5 cm) wide, for valance
- 2 yd. (1.85 m) lightweight to mediumweight fabric, up to 54" (137 cm) wide, or 1 yd. (0.95 m) of 60" (152.5 cm) fabric, for curtains
- 1½ yd. (1.4 m) dark or mediumweight to heavyweight fabric, 60" (152.5 cm) wide, for stage panel
- 1½ yd. (1.4 m) ribbon, 1" (2.5 cm) wide
- Clear vinyl sheeting, 9½" × 12" (24.3 × 30.5 cm)
- Extra-wide double-fold bias tape
- Thread to match fabrics
- Glue stick
- Ten clip-on or sew-on curtain rings
- Three spring-tension rods to fit doorway

Tools:

- Sewing machine
- Fabric scissors
- Iron
- Straightedge
- Hand needle

The audience waits in eager anticipation. Finally, the curtain opens, and the show begins! A magical stage for make-believe, this easy-to-sew puppet theater provides kids with hours of fun. With the use of spring-pressure rods, it is quickly installed in any doorway measuring 30" to 36" (76 to 91.5 cm) wide. Puppeteers and stagehands crouch unseen behind the stage panel, acting out stories with their hands. A pocket on the back of the stage panel keeps puppets and props at hand. Show announcements slide in and out of the clear pocket on the front. After the show, the theater folds flat or rolls up for storage.

Select mediumweight fabric with cheerful, bright colors for the curtains and valance of your puppet theater. For the lower stage panel, select a heavier opaque fabric that will hide the performers well.

Builds imagination
Portable
Folds flat for storage

1 Cut the valance fabric 15" (38 cm) long, the full width of the fabric. Cut two pieces of fabric for the curtains, each 30" (76 cm) long and 25" (63.5 cm) wide. Cut fabric for the stage panel 45" (115 cm) long and 44" (112 cm) wide. Cut fabric for back pocket 12" × 54" (30.5 × 137 cm).

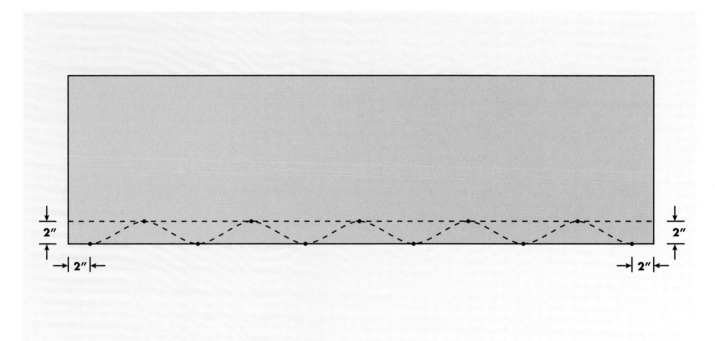

2 Sew valance pieces together as necessary. On wrong side, mark 2" (5 cm) from each end at lower edge. Divide remaining distance into five equal spaces; mark. Draw a line 2" (5 cm) above lower edge; make marks on upper line midway between lower marks.

3 Connect marks with smoothly curving line. If desired, make a template and trace repeatedly across the lower edge. Cut on the curved line.

4 Encase curved lower edge between folds of double-fold bias tape, with the shorter side of the tape on the right side of the valance. Shape tape to fit curves smoothly by steaming. Glue-baste in place. Stitch close to folded edge on right side.

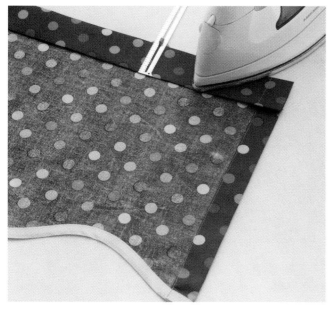

5 Stitch 1" (2.5 cm) double-fold hems on valance ends. Press top edge under ½" (1.3 cm), then press under 2" (5 cm) to form rod pocket.

6 Press a 1" (2.5 cm) double-fold hem in the lower edge of each curtain panel; stitch. Repeat for sides and tops. Attach five sew-on or clip-on rings, evenly spaced across the top of each panel, placing the end rings at the side hems.

7 Press and stitch ½" (1.3 cm) double-fold hem in back pocket top. Fold pocket in half sideways, right sides together. Stitch 2" (5 cm) from fold, 2" (5 cm) from lower edge. Open pleat; press flat. (continued)

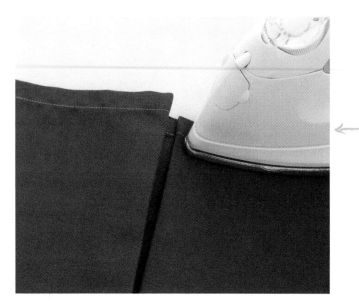

8 Fold in outer edge 10½" (26.7 cm), right sides together. Stitch 2" (5 cm) from fold, 2" (5 cm) from lower edge. Repeat for opposite side. Open pleats; press flat.

9 Press under ½" (1.3 cm) at bottom of pocket. Center pocket on wrong side of stage panel. Baste side edges in place 1" (2.5 cm) from edges of panel. Topstitch bottom; topstitch halfway between pleats to form pockets.

10 Cut two pieces of ribbon 10½" (26.7 cm) long. Center ribbon on short side of vinyl, overlapping ½" (1.3 cm); topstitch, using slightly long stitch. Repeat on opposite side.

11 Cut two pieces of ribbon 1" (2.5 cm) longer than the long edge of vinyl pocket, including the ribbon border. Press under ½" (1.3 cm) at each end of both pieces. Center ribbons on long edges, overlapping edge by ½" (1.3 cm) and enclosing side ribbons. Topstitch in place.

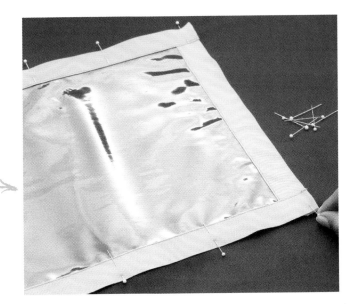

12 Place clear pocket over stage panel front, covering stitches from center back pocket; pin. Stitch close to ribbon edges on three sides, leaving one short end open. Backstitch to secure.

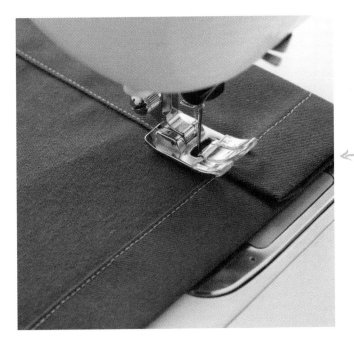

13 Press and stitch 1" (2.5 cm) double-fold hems on stage panel sides; repeat for bottom. Press top edge under ½" (1.3 cm), then press under 2" (5 cm) to form rod pocket; stitch.

14 Adjust tension rods to fit in doorway. Insert tension rods into rod pockets of valance and stage; insert remaining rod through rings of curtains. Mount stage panel and curtain in doorway, overlapping 4" to 5" (10 to 12.7 cm); adjust height as necessary. Mount valance above curtain.

Dramatic Style

To give the theater a more dramatic look, use velour fabric and stitch decorator trim to the valance edge instead of bias tape.

Puppets and props are kept at hand on the back of the stage panel, so puppeteers can make quick changes.

To store the theater, place the puppets and props into the back pockets. Remove the spring tension rods, fold up the curtains and valance, and place them over the center pocket. Fold in the bottom and top thirds of the stage. Fold into thirds from side to side and tie with a ribbon.

Diagram for Folding Up the Puppet Theater

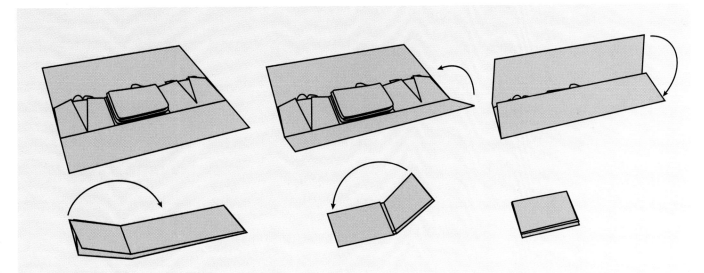

Collapse the tent for easy storage, wrapping it like an umbrella and securing it at the bottom with the attached shoelace.

Recommended for ages: 1 — 10

Price Range: $5 — $50

Time to Complete: 1 hour — 5 hours

PLAYHOUSE TENTS

This tent serves as either an indoor or outdoor playhouse. Supported by four ¾" (2 cm) PVC pipes, the tent can be erected quickly and easily by a child and stores compactly. The PVC pipe, available from hardware stores, is inexpensive, easy to cut, and very durable. A generous 54" (137 cm) on each side, the tent is large enough to share with friends.

For comfort, make the tent from cotton poplin or other mediumweight cotton fabric. Nylon fabric may also be used, but it will be hotter inside the tent. To add interest, select a bright-colored striped fabric for the casings.

Materials:

- 4½ yd. (4.15 m) fabric, 54" (137 cm) or wider, for the primary tent fabric
- ⅞ yd. (0.8 m) fabric, 45" (115 cm) or wider, for the casing strips
- Four 68" (173 cm) lengths of ¾" (2 cm) PVC pipe
- Eight end caps for ¾" (2 cm) PVC pipe or for 1" (2.5 cm) chair legs
- One pair of shoelaces, 36" (91.5 cm) long
- Two squares of hook and loop tape
- Paper for drawing patterns

Tools:

Straightedge

Fabric scissors

Iron

Sewing machine

Drill; ³⁄₁₆" drill bit

PVC pipe cutter or hacksaw and sandpaper

Acetone and soft cloth; rubber gloves

Opens instantly
Easy to store

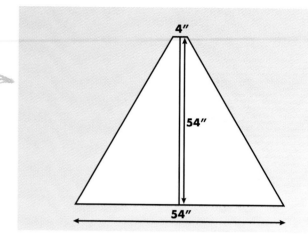

1 Draw 54" (137 cm) line on large piece of paper, for bottom of tent section. From center of this line, draw a perpendicular 54" (137 cm) line; draw 4" (10 cm) horizontal line, centered at top of this line. Connect ends of 4" (10 cm) line to ends of bottom line. This trapezoid is the pattern for three sides of tent.

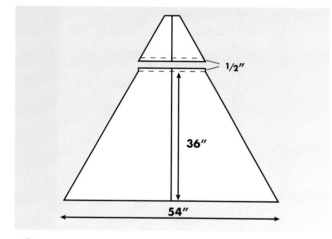

2 Draw a second trapezoid same size as in step 1; cut this trapezoid parallel to and 36" (91.5 cm) from bottom line. Add ½" (1.3 cm) seam allowances to edges where trapezoid was cut apart. Small trapezoid is pattern for upper front section.

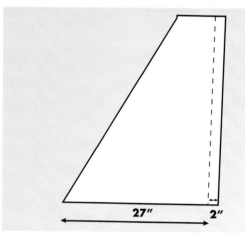

3 Fold bottom portion from step 2 in half lengthwise; crease. Unfold, and draw a line, parallel to and 2" (5 cm) from crease; cut on line, and discard smaller piece. Larger piece is pattern for lower front sections.

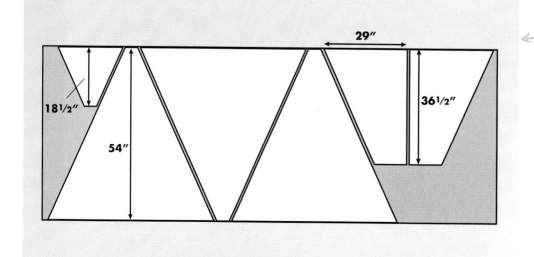

4 Cut three sides, one upper front, and two lower front sections, using patterns drawn in steps 1 to 3; for efficient use of the fabric, cut the pieces on the crosswise grain with bottoms of pieces on the selvages. For the casings, cut 5" (12.7 cm) fabric strips on crosswise grain; piece the strips together as necessary to make four 5" × 58" (12.7 × 147 cm) casing strips.

5 Press under ¼" (6 mm) twice on vertical side of two lower fronts; stitch to make double-fold hems. Repeat for hems on lower edges. Overlap the two lower fronts 3" (7.5 cm); pin.

6 Align top edge of lapped lower front sections to bottom edge of upper front section, with pieces right sides together. Stitch ½" (1.3 cm) seam; finish the seam, using zigzag stitch.

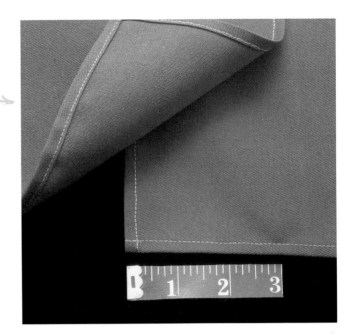

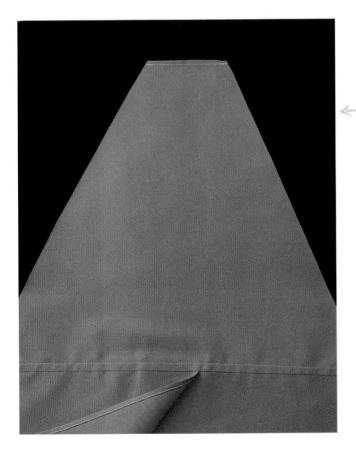

7 Press seam toward upper front section. Top-stitch ⅜" (1 cm) from seam. Press and stitch ¼" (6 mm) double-fold hem on upper edge of front section.

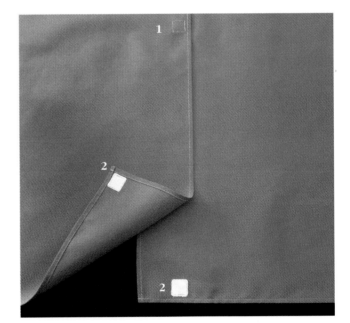

8 Position squares of hook and loop tape at center of lower front opening (1) and near lower edge (2). Stitch in place. (continued)

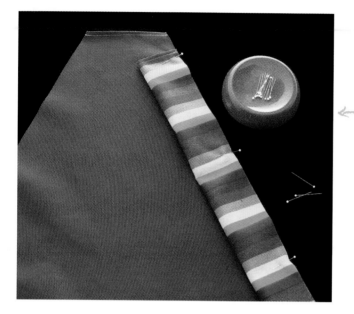

9 Press and stitch ¼" (6 mm) double-fold hems on top and bottom edges of all remaining tent sections and on short ends of casing strips.

10 Fold a casing strip in half lengthwise, wrong sides together. Center folded casing strip on one diagonal edge of front section, with right sides together and raw edges even; pin.

11 Place one side section of tent over the front section, right sides together, matching diagonal edges. Repin through all layers. Stitch ½" (1.3 cm) seam; finish seam, using zigzag stitch.

12 Apply remaining casings and stitch remaining diagonal seams of tent as in steps 10 and 11.

13 Pin one shoelace to outside of tent back section, centering it 3" (7.5 cm) from the lower edge. Stitch through the center of the shoelace for 2" (5 cm), using multistitch-zigzag.

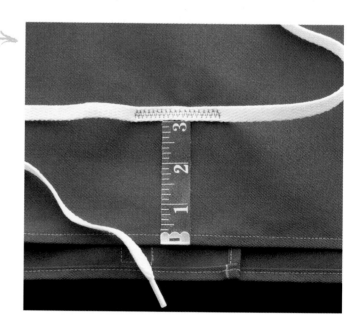

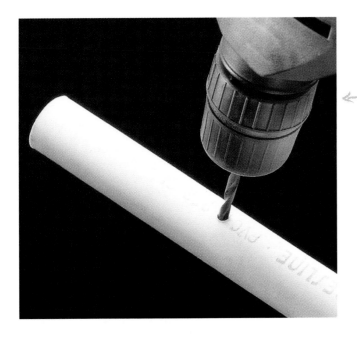

14 Drill hole completely through each PVC pipe, 4" (10 cm) from upper end, using ³/₁₆" drill bit.

15 Remove any labeling or other markings from the PVC pipes, using acetone and a soft cloth; wear rubber gloves.

Hint: Tape a toothpick to the shoelace end for easier threading.

16 Slide PVC pipes into casings, with holes at top of tent; apply end caps to top and bottom of each pipe.

17 Thread remaining shoelace through holes in the PVC pipes as shown; knot securely. To erect tent, spread the pipes apart at bottom of tent and arrange them as shown on page 52.

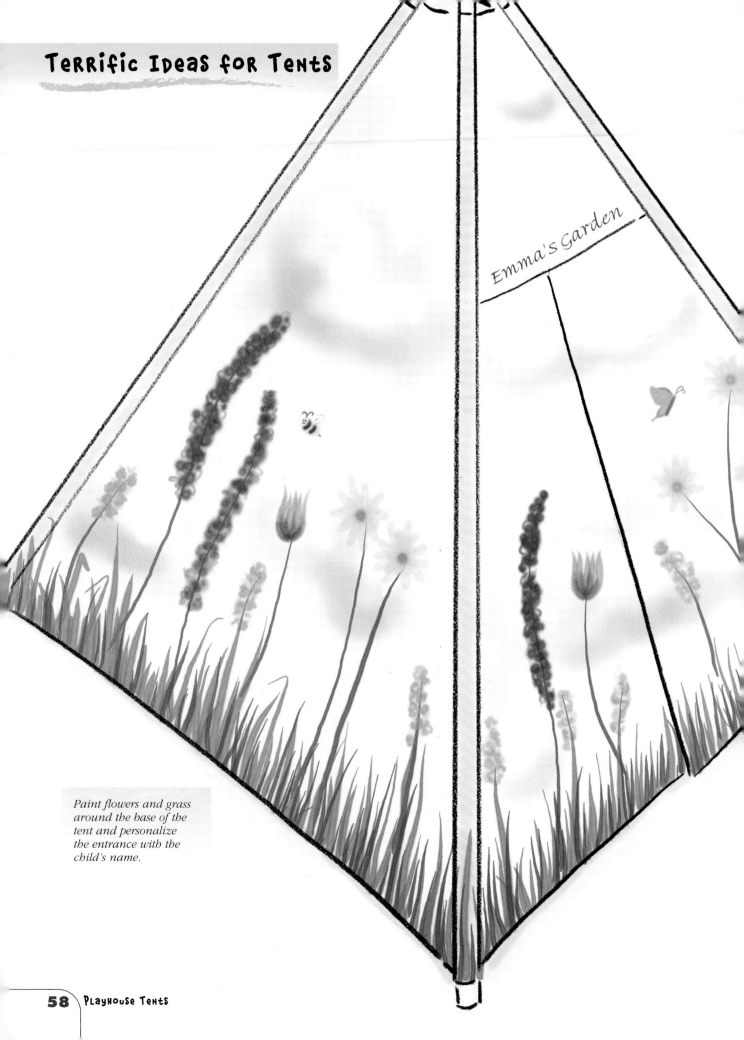

Terrific Ideas for Tents

Emma's Garden

Paint flowers and grass around the base of the tent and personalize the entrance with the child's name.

Add circular netting windows to three sides of the tent before sewing it together. Draw a 9" (23 cm) circle on the netting; pin it to the outside of the tent piece in the upper half. Stitch the circle to the fabric, using a short, narrow zigzag stitch. Trim the excess netting up to the stitching. From the back, trim the fabric away from the inside of the circle, taking care not to cut the netting.

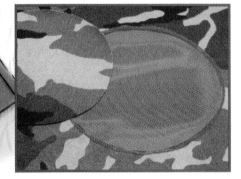

Tie glow-in-the-dark balls, stars, or other items to shoelaces at the top of the tent. When playing with the tent, suspend the items inside as "ceiling lights." When not in use, hang the items on the outside to recharge the glow.

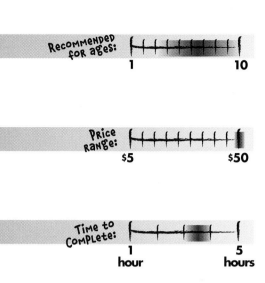

LITTLE ARTIST'S EASEL

Materials:

- Four 60" (152.5 cm) lengths of 1" (2.5 cm) PVC pipe
- Six tee fittings for 1" (2.5 cm) pipe
- Two elbows for 1" (2.5 cm) pipe
- PVC cement
- 18" (46 cm) chain; two cup hooks
- 24" (61 cm) square of ¼" (6 mm) MDF board
- Aerosol chalkboard paint
- 24" (61 cm) square of ¼" (6 mm) acrylic
- Eight #10 × 1" (2.5 cm) pan-head wood screws
- Two Rubbermaid® Slide'n Stack™ plastic baskets
- Plastic window screen clips; screws
- Four rubber end caps to fit pipe
- Two binder clips or colorful clothespins

Tools:

- PVC pipe cutter or hacksaw and sandpaper
- Acetone and soft cloth; rubber gloves
- Rubber mallet
- Fine-tooth file; sandpaper
- Drill and drill bits
- Screwdriver; pliers

Encourage the budding artist with this sturdy, multipurpose easel. The frame, made from PVC pipe, supports a clear acrylic painting board on one side and a chalkboard on the other. Kids can paint directly on the washable acrylic board or clip art paper to the board when they want to save their creations. The opposite side of the easel holds a chalkboard, created by painting MDF board with chalkboard paint.

PVC pipe is available in the plumbing section of home improvement centers and hardware stores. The size printed on the pipe refers to the inside diameter of the pipe. Markings can be removed with acetone and a soft cloth.

Most of the pipe sections need not be glued together; they fit very snugly when pounded with a rubber mallet. Only the lower crossbars are glued in place so they will not rotate under the weight of the trays. Once the boards have been attached, the horizontal joints cannot separate. The top joints, however, are free to rotate, so that the easel can be collapsed for storage.

FOLDS flat to store
STURDY CONSTRUCTION
Easy to clean

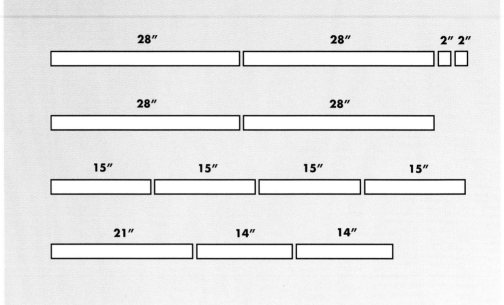

1 Clean PVC pipes. Carefully measure and mark these cut lengths for the pieces as indicated in the diagram: four 28" (71 cm), four 15" (38 cm), two 14" (35.5 cm), one 21" (53.5 cm), and two 2" (5 cm). Cut pieces, using a PVC pipe cutter for a clean, even cut. Or use a hacksaw and sand the edges smooth.

2 Connect 28" (71 cm) upper legs and 15" (38 cm) lower legs to tee fittings. Connect front legs at tees with 21" (53.5 cm) lower crossbar; connect back legs with 14" (35.5 cm) lower crossbar. Glue crossbar joints, using multi-purpose cement; place legs on flat surface to be sure they are parallel. Pound sections together securely, using a rubber mallet.

3 Form upper crossbar, using two elbows, two 2" (5 cm) pipe sections, two tee fittings, and 14" (35.5 cm) section; pound together securely. Join front and back legs to upper crossbar; pound together securely.

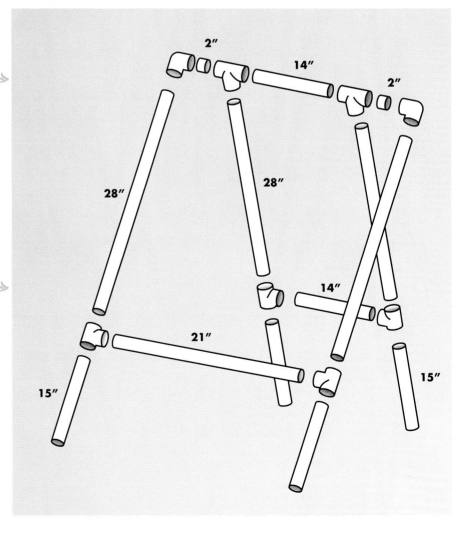

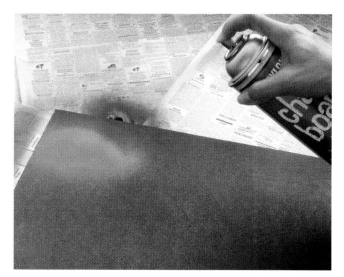

4. Round acrylic board corners smooth with fine file. Sand any rough or sharp edges smooth. Paint MDF board, using chalkboard paint; follow manufacturer's directions. Allow to dry completely.

5. Center acrylic board on front legs, just below top elbows. Mark locations for screw holes in board, ½" (1.3 cm) from top and bottom edges. Mark corresponding locations on legs. Repeat for MDF board and back legs.

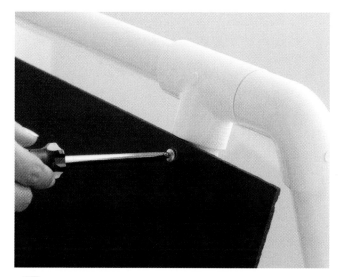

6. Drill holes in boards, using drill bit slightly *larger* than screws. Drill holes in legs, using drill bit slightly *smaller* than screws. Secure boards to legs, using hand screwdriver.

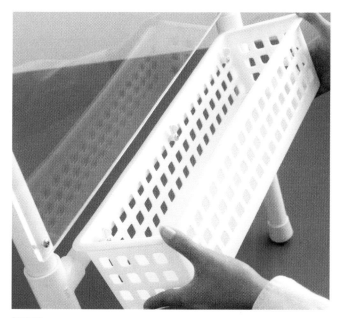

7. Attach three or four window screen clips to lower crossbar, aligning placement to holes in basket. Hang basket on clips. Repeat for opposite side.

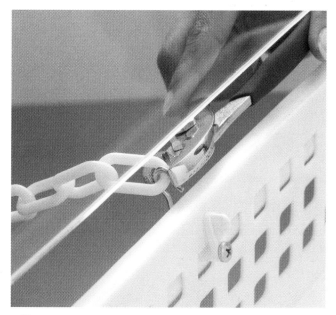

8. Secure chain to center top of lower crossbars, using cup hooks. (Predrill holes slightly smaller than cup hook screws.) Close cup hooks, using pliers.

9. Attach rubber end caps to ends of legs. Attach binder clips to upper edge of acrylic paint board.

Having Fun with the Little Artist's Easel

Design the easel to fit the interests of your kids. Attach acrylic boards to both sides if you have two avid painters. Perhaps a pegboard and oodles of colored golf tees are more appealing than a chalkboard. Here are some other ideas for playing with an artist's easel:

Use the acrylic board to play with cling vinyl shapes. Purchase precut shapes, such as Colorforms®, or cut your own shapes from cling vinyl sheets sold in assorted colors.

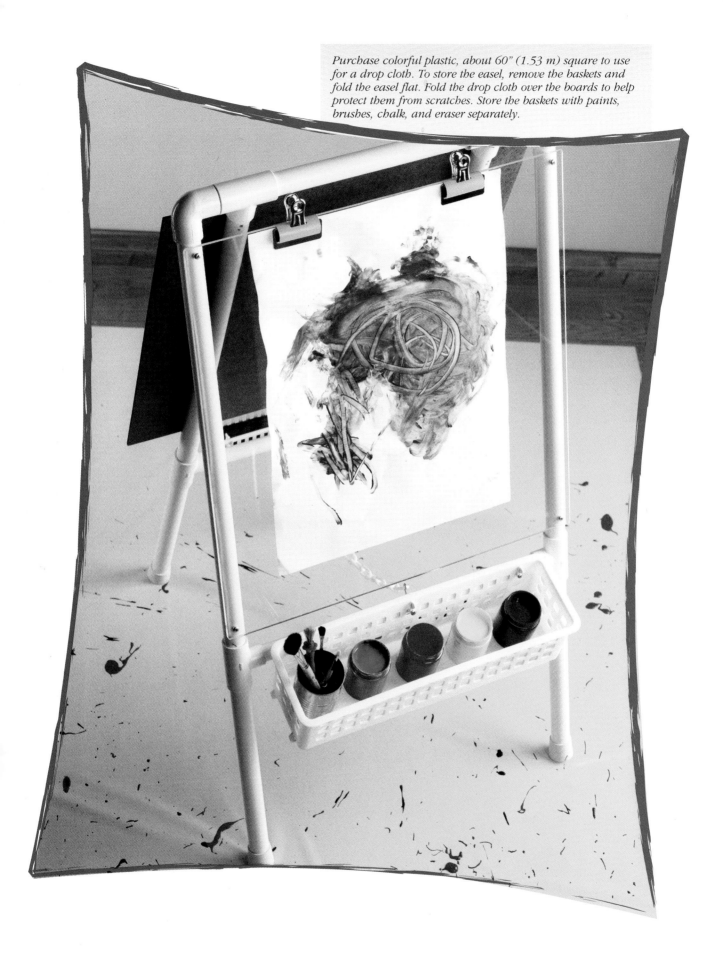

Purchase colorful plastic, about 60" (1.53 m) square to use for a drop cloth. To store the easel, remove the baskets and fold the easel flat. Fold the drop cloth over the boards to help protect them from scratches. Store the baskets with paints, brushes, chalk, and eraser separately.

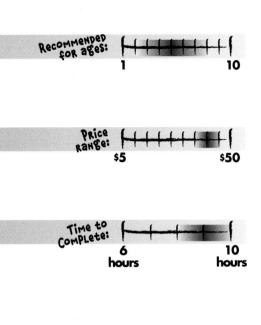

Recommended for ages: 1 — 10

Price range: $5 — $50

Time to Complete: 6 hours — 10 hours

Easy to clean

Sturdy construction

Affordable

Coloring, cutting, drawing, printing, playing board games, modeling clay, and snacking are just a few of the activities that call for a table and chairs. This pint-size set is just right for little people with short legs. The chairs are lightweight but sturdy; the fabric seats and backs are attached to frames made of inexpensive PVC pipe. A wooden tabletop is attached to wide PVC pipe legs that offer stable support.

The PVC pipes fit the joints very tightly, so gluing is not necessary. The seat and back can be removed for laundering, if needed, simply by pounding the joints apart with a rubber mallet. Nylon canvas seats and backs can be washed clean while still on the frame.

Materials:

For two chairs:

¾ yd. (0.7 m) nylon canvas; thread

Five 60" (152.5 cm) lengths of ¾" (2 cm) PVC pipe

Sixteen elbows for ¾" (2 cm) pipe

Sixteen tee fittings for ¾" (2 cm) pipe

For table:

30" (76 cm) plywood square, ¾" (2 cm) thick, for tabletop

Iron-on veneer edging

Latex paint or wood stain and clear acrylic finish

72" (183 cm) length of 1½" (3.8 cm) PVC pipe

Eight end caps for 1½" (3.8 cm) pipe

Twelve #8 × ¾" (2 cm) flat-head wood screws

Adhesive-back felt to pad table leg ends, optional

Tools:

Fabric scissors

Sewing machine

Iron

PVC pipe cutter, or hacksaw and sandpaper

Rubber mallet

Acetone and soft cloth; rubber gloves

Drill and drill bits; screwdriver

Sandpaper; tack cloth

Veneer edge trimmer

Paintbrush

1 Cut the chair seat 12½" × 22½" (31.8 × 57 cm); cut the chair back 12" × 15" (30.5 × 38 cm). Press a ¼" (6 mm) double-fold hem in the long ends of each piece; stitch.

2 Fold under short ends of seat ½" (1.3 cm); press. Fold under again 3" (7.5 cm). Stitch along folded edge, forming casing. Stitch again ¼" (6 mm) from first stitching. Reinforce stitches, using short narrow zigzag at ends.

3 Pin short ends of back, right sides together. Stitch ½" (1.3 cm) seam. Trim seam allowances, and finish seam allowances together. Turn right side out.

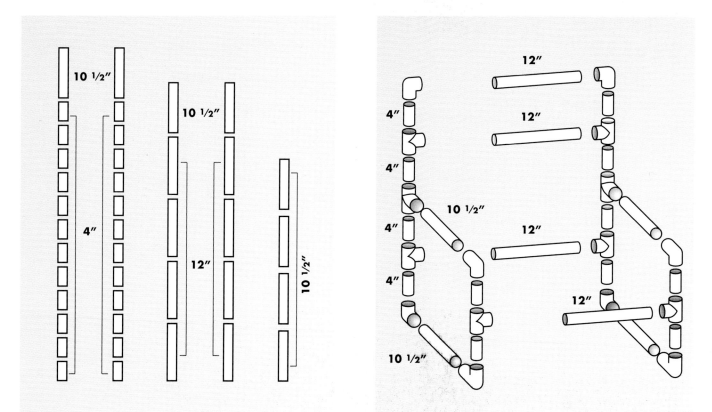

4 Clean pipes, using acetone and a soft cloth; wear rubber gloves. Carefully measure and mark these cut lengths for the pieces as indicated in the diagram: eight 10½" (26.7 cm), eight 12" (30.5 cm), and twenty-four 4" (10 cm). Cut pieces, using PVC pipe cutter for a clean, even cut. Or use a hacksaw and sand the edges smooth. These measurements are for a chair seat height of 12" (30.5 cm). See the suggestions and chart on page 71 to adjust the height.

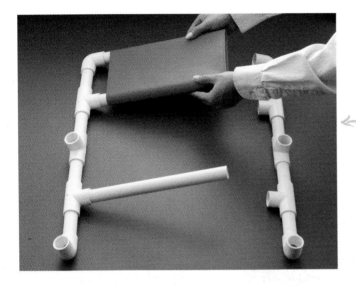

5 Connect elbows, tee fittings, and pipe pieces to make the back of the chair. Insert 12" (30.5 cm) pipes through fabric back before connecting to elbows and back tee fittings.

6 Connect elbows, tee fittings, and pipe pieces to make the seat and front legs of the chair. Insert two 10½" (26.7 cm) pieces through seat casings.

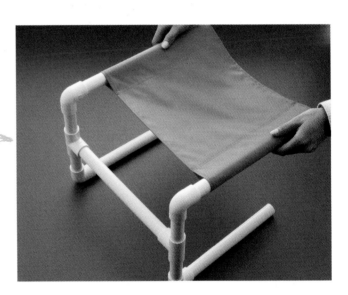

7 Connect the seat and front legs to the chair back. Pound all pipes securely into fittings, using a rubber mallet, beginning with vertical connections. Turn chair on its side and back to pound horizontal connections.

1 Predrill three holes, evenly spaced, near the inner edge of four end caps; countersink holes slightly using a larger bit. Place caps 1½" (3.8 cm) from the edges at each corner, on the underside of the table. Predrill shallow pilot holes in table; secure caps to table.

2 Cut 1½" (3.8 cm) PVC pipe into four 18" (46 cm) table legs. Pound legs into end caps, using rubber mallet. Pound remaining end caps onto ends of table legs. Apply adhesive felt circles to end caps, if desired.

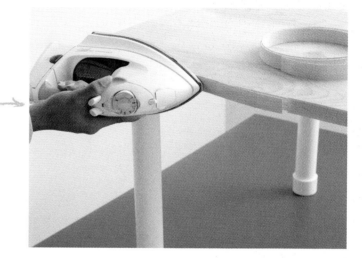

3 Sand entire tabletop until smooth. Wipe with tack cloth. Apply veneer edging to the edge of the tabletop, centering it on the edge. Follow the manufacturer's directions.

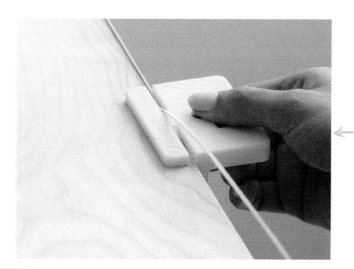

4 Trim away excess edging, using an edge trimmer; sand edging lightly. Paint or stain and finish tabletop as desired.

Personalize the table and chairs with the child's handprints and name. Brush acrylic paint onto the child's palm to make the handprints; use paint pens to write names. For longer life, finish the painted tabletop with a coat of polyurethane. To personalize the chair, use cotton canvas for the seat and back and add the handprints and name with fabric paints and paint pens.

As kids grow, table legs can be replaced inexpensively, and the ten PVC pieces that make up the chair legs and lower part of the chair back can be replaced with slightly longer ones. As a general rule, there should be a space of 6" to 10" (15 to 25.5 cm) between the chair seat and the tabletop. Use the chart at the right to adjust the height of the table and chairs to suit the size of your kids.

Age	2-3	4-5	6-7	8-9
Standard Seat Height	10" (25.5 cm)	12" (30.5 cm)	14" (35.5 cm)	16" (40.5 cm)
Eight Short Pieces in Chair Legs	3" (7.5 cm)	4" (10 cm)	5" (12.7 cm)	6" (15 cm)
Two Short Pieces in Lower Chair Back	4" (10 cm)	4" (10 cm)	5" (12.7 cm)	6" (15 cm)
Length of Table Legs	16" (40.5 cm)	18" (46 cm)	20" (51 cm)	22" (56 cm)

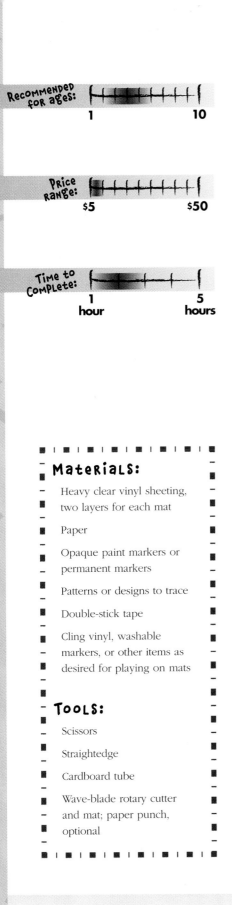

SEE-THROUGH PLAY MATS

Recommended for ages: 1 — 10

Price Range: $5 — $50

Time to Complete: 1 hour — 5 hours

Clear vinyl table covers can be designed to suit a variety of activities. Guidelines, shapes, and drawings are applied to vinyl and covered with another piece of vinyl, so kids can play over and over on the wipe-clean surface. Made from heavy vinyl sheeting, the mats can be cut to the size of the kid's table or any tabletop, so they protect the table surface while the kids are having fun. When not in use, small mats can be stacked and hung from a hanger with clips. Larger mats can be rolled on cardboard tubes.

Materials:

- Heavy clear vinyl sheeting, two layers for each mat
- Paper
- Opaque paint markers or permanent markers
- Patterns or designs to trace
- Double-stick tape
- Cling vinyl, washable markers, or other items as desired for playing on mats

Tools:

- Scissors
- Straightedge
- Cardboard tube
- Wave-blade rotary cutter and mat; paper punch, optional

Easy to make

Endless possibilities

Wipe-clean surface

Paint a checkerboard in the center of the mat. Around the edges, draw grids for ticktacktoe or other simple games. Trace from favorite coloring books or royalty-free picture books for outlined pictures to be colored in again and again.

1 Cut two pieces of vinyl about 2" (5 cm) larger than the desired finished size. Mark finished size and draw designs on paper pattern. Place one vinyl piece over pattern. Draw design on vinyl, using paint pens or permanent markers. Allow to dry completely.

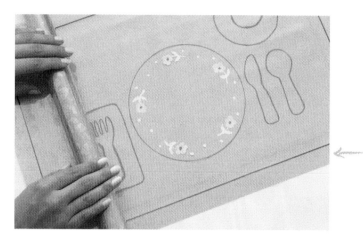

2 Adhere double-stick tape to border of painted vinyl, following marked line on pattern. Roll remaining vinyl piece onto cardboard tube. Unroll over painted piece, smoothing them together and sealing the border. Cut mat to size, using rotary cutter or scissors. Punch holes along border, if desired.

Creative Play Mat Ideas

For a dainty tea party mat, cut the outer edge of the mat with a wave-blade rotary cutter. Draw the place settings for a tea party, with figures showing the placement of the plates, silverware, cups, and napkins. Kids can set play dishes and a centerpiece on the table along with the tea.

Design a clay-play surface. Paint circles, squares, rectangles, and triangles in various sizes. Paint basic body shapes for kids to dress and accessorize with clay. Draw a swarm of bugs and other critters that kids can make from clay balls, ropes, and other shapes.

(continued)

Creative Play Mat Ideas

(CONTINUED)

Copy the alphabet and numbers on these pages; trace them on the mat. Draw extra lines 1" (2.5 cm) apart with a dotted line down the center for kids to practice their printing skills, spelling words, or simple arithmetic.

Alphabet & Number Patterns

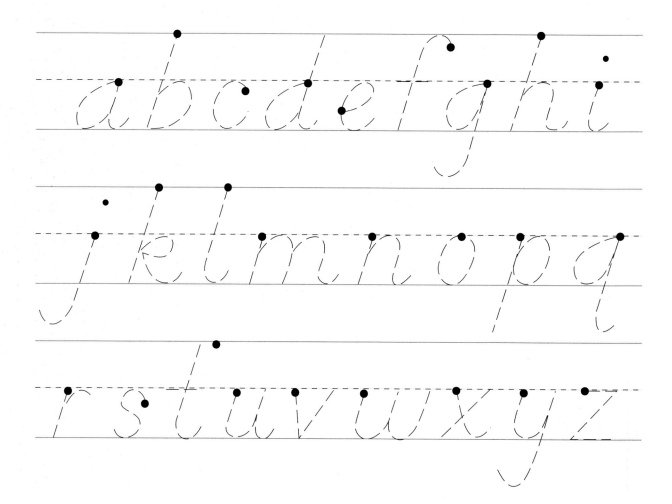

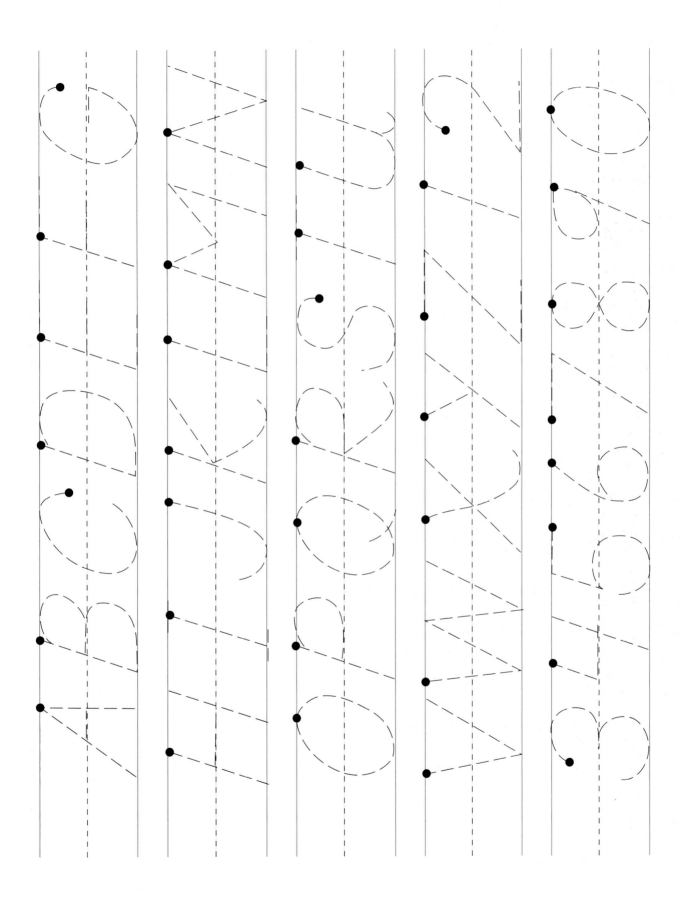

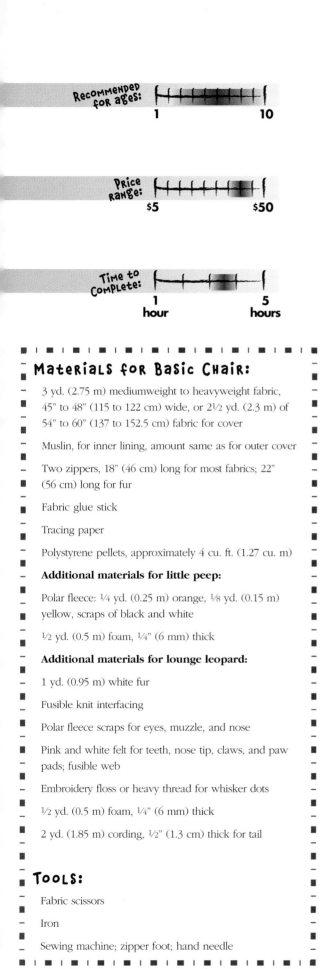

Recommended for ages:

1 — 10

Price range:

$5 — $50

Time to Complete:

1 hour — 5 hours

Materials for Basic Chair:

- 3 yd. (2.75 m) mediumweight to heavyweight fabric, 45" to 48" (115 to 122 cm) wide, or 2½ yd. (2.3 m) of 54" to 60" (137 to 152.5 cm) fabric for cover

- Muslin, for inner lining, amount same as for outer cover

- Two zippers, 18" (46 cm) long for most fabrics; 22" (56 cm) long for fur

- Fabric glue stick

- Tracing paper

- Polystyrene pellets, approximately 4 cu. ft. (1.27 cu. m)

Additional materials for little peep:

- Polar fleece: ¼ yd. (0.25 m) orange, ⅛ yd. (0.15 m) yellow, scraps of black and white

- ½ yd. (0.5 m) foam, ¼" (6 mm) thick

Additional materials for lounge leopard:

- 1 yd. (0.95 m) white fur

- Fusible knit interfacing

- Polar fleece scraps for eyes, muzzle, and nose

- Pink and white felt for teeth, nose tip, claws, and paw pads; fusible web

- Embroidery floss or heavy thread for whisker dots

- ½ yd. (0.5 m) foam, ¼" (6 mm) thick

- 2 yd. (1.85 m) cording, ½" (1.3 cm) thick for tail

Tools:

- Fabric scissors

- Iron

- Sewing machine; zipper foot; hand needle

BEANBAG CHAIRS

For lounging in front of the television, curling up to read a book, or settling in for a cozy afternoon nap, nothing beats the comfort of a plump beanbag chair. Although the name implies that the bag is filled with beans, it is actually filled with polystyrene pellets, making the chair lightweight and moldable. With a clever selection of fabrics and the addition of a few details, these child-size beanbag chairs can be sewn to look like a beach ball or friendly animal pals.

The beanbag chair consists of a zippered muslin inner lining, which holds the pellets, and a zippered outer cover. For the outer cover, select a mediumweight fabric, such as synthetic fur, denim, canvas, wide-wale corduroy, or upholstery fabric.

Snuggly soft

Saves money

Cute as can be

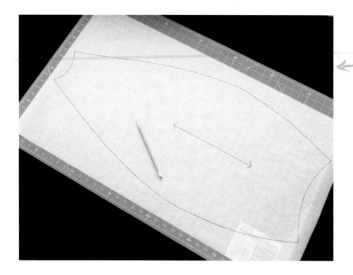

1. Place tracing paper over a 1" (2.5 cm) grid. Make full-size pattern for sides of chair, using the diagram on page 85 as a guide. Cut six side pieces each from fabric and lining. For the chair top, cut one circle each from fabric and lining, with the radius equal to 4½" (11.5 cm).

2. Fold a piece of paper, at least 20" (51 cm) square, in half; make a mark at center of fold. Using straightedge and pencil, mark arc on paper measuring 10" (25.5 cm) from the marked point. Cut on marked line.

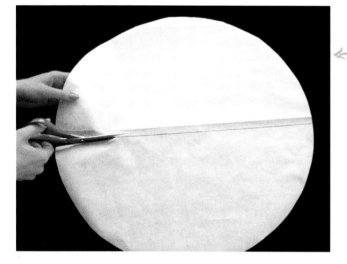

3. Unfold paper; mark a line ½" (1.3 cm) from fold. Cut on marked line, and discard smallest piece of circle; remainder of circle is pattern for bottom of chair. Cut two chair bottom pieces each from fabric and lining, aligning the straight edges to the lengthwise grain of the fabric.

4. Pin chair bottom pieces together along straight edges. Machine-baste a ½" (1.3 cm) seam; using a regular stitch length, stitch at the ends of seam for 1" (2.5 cm). Press seam open.

5. Center zipper right side down over seam allowances. Glue-baste in place, using glue stick. Stitch down each side of zipper tape ¼" (6 mm) from zipper teeth. Remove basting stitches.

6. Stitch long edges of side pieces, right sides together, in ½" (1.3 cm) seam; leave last seam unstitched. Press seam allowances to one side, pressing all in same direction.

7 Topstitch ⅜" (1 cm) from seams. Stitch remaining seam; press seam allowances to one side, and topstitch.

8 Staystitch upper edge of bag a scant ½" (1.3 cm) from edge. From raw edge, clip seam allowance at ½" (1.3 cm) intervals. Divide the outer edge of top circle into six parts; mark. Pin the upper edge of bag to top circle, right sides together, matching seams of sides to marks on circle. Stitch ½" (1.3 cm) seam.

9 Press seam allowances toward the bag sides; topstitch ⅜" (1 cm) from the seam. Repeat step 8 for the bag bottom, leaving zipper partially opened.

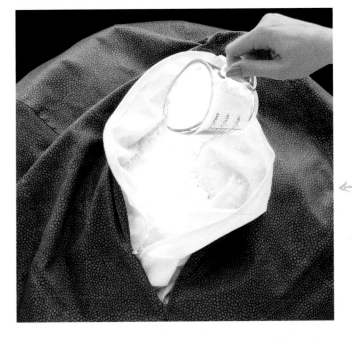

10 Turn bag right side out through the zipper opening. Press the bottom seam allowances toward bag sides; topstitch ⅜" (1 cm) from seam.

11 Repeat steps 4 to 10 for inner lining. Insert the lining into outer cover; fill the bag with polystyrene pellets. Close zippers.

How to Sew a Little Peep Beanbag Chair

1 Follow steps 1 to 3, page 80. Open the zipper; place one side face-down on the right side of one circle half, with edge of teeth ¾" (2 cm) from fabric edge and upper zipper stop ⅝" (1.5 cm) from outer curve. Allow bottom of zipper to extend beyond curved edge. Stitch ½" (1.3 cm) from fabric edge. Repeat for opposite side of zipper.

2 Cut out white and black polar fleece eye pieces. Glue-baste black pieces to white pieces; stitch close to inside curved edge with a short straight stitch. Glue-baste eyes to top circle, following pattern guideline. Stitch close to outer edges to secure.

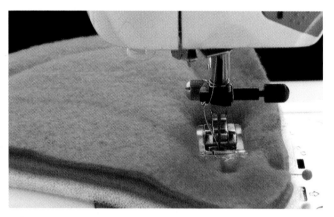

3 Cut two pieces of orange polar fleece and a piece of foam about 1" (2.5 cm) larger all around than beak pattern, page 87. Trace pattern on wrong side of fabric. Place pieces right sides together, with traced piece on top. Place pieces over foam; pin. Stitch on marked line, leaving inner curve open.

5 Cut yellow polar fleece strip 2½" × 16" (6.5 × 40.5 cm). Cut fringe every ¼" (6 mm) to within ¾" (2 cm) of long edge. Fold in half twice; baste layers together, forming head tuft. Cut second strip 3½" × 24" (9 × 61 cm); cut fringe. Fold in half three times; baste layers together, forming tail feathers.

6 Baste wings to opposite sides of two front sections, 12" (30.5 cm) from upper edge. Baste tail feathers to center back seam allowance, 6" (15 cm) from bottom. Follow steps 6 and 7 on pages 80 and 81, omitting topstitching. Baste beak to top center of front, aligning point to seam; clip beak seam allowance to fit curve. Baste head tuft to top center of back. Baste feet to bottom centers of two front sections.

7 Finish chair, following steps 8 to 11 on page 81, omitting topstitching. When attaching bottom circle, stitch carefully across zipper teeth that extend into seam allowance.

4 Trim the curved opening to ½" (1.3 cm); trim the remaining seam allowances to ¼" (6 mm). Turn beak right side out, using blunt point, such as eraser end of a pencil or chopstick, to push out point. Prepare orange polar fleece feet and yellow fur wings, following steps for beak.

1 Follow steps 1 to 3 on page 80. Cut five chair sections of leopard print; cut one of white fur. Fuse interfacing to wrong side of fabric before cutting top circle. Using the patterns on pages 87 to 89, cut one brow from fused leopard print; cut two ear centers, two tufts, two beards, and a 5" (12.7 cm) square for tail tip from white fur. Cut two white eyes, one muzzle, and one nose from white polar fleece. Cut two navy blue polar fleece eyes and a medium blue polar fleece nose. From unfused leopard print, cut eight paws, four ears, and a 5" × 31" (12.7 × 78.5 cm) strip for tail.

2 Fuse two white felt squares together, using fusible web. From white felt, cut four teeth and sixteen claws. From pink felt, cut one mouth, one nose tip, two foot pads, and eight toe pads.

3 Follow steps 4 and 5, page 80 for inserting the zipper on suede or short pile fabric. Use zipper insertion method in step 1, opposite, for longer fur.

4 Appliqué face pieces in order as they are numbered in the diagram on page 88. Glue-baste and edgestitch pieces in place one at a time. Overlap pieces as indicated in the diagram. Use short narrow zigzag stitch around brow. Hand-embroider French knots on cheeks.

5 Appliqué white center to ear, using short, narrow zigzag stitch. Stitch two ear pieces right sides together on seamline; trim. Turn right side out. Baste to face circle at placement marks, ³⁄₈" (1 cm) from edge.

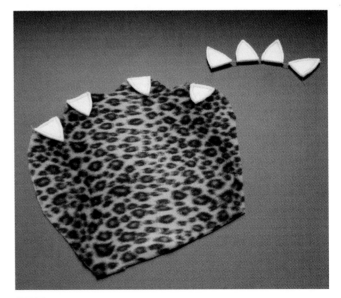

6 Stitch tuft pieces, right sides together on seamline; trim. Turn right side out. Repeat for beard. Baste tuft and beard to face circle at placement marks, ³⁄₈" (1 cm) from edge.

7 Stitch close to cut edges on two sides of each claw, stitching all claws continuously; clip apart. Baste claws to toes, with points facing inward. Appliqué pads on two paws. (continued)

8 Cut four pieces of foam slightly larger than paw pattern. Place paws, right sides together over foam (appliquéd side underneath); pin. Stitch on seamline, leaving straight end open. Trim seam allowance; clip corners. Turn right side out. Repeat for remaining paws.

9 Stitch tail end to tail, right sides together. Press seam allowances open. Cut foam strip 5" × 35" (12.7 × 89 cm). Pin to wrong side of tail; baste within ½" (1.3 cm) seam allowance. Measure distance from one end of cording to cut length of tail, minus 1½" (3.8 cm); mark.

10 Fold strip over cording; right sides together, placing one end of strip at mark on cording and extending fabric away from short end of cord. Pin together long edges of tail.

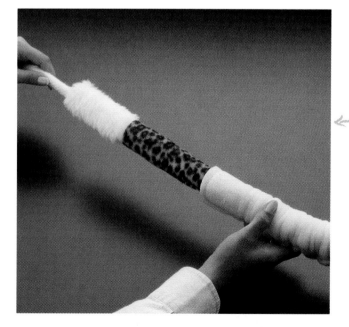

11 Stitch ½" (1.3 cm) from long edges, taking care not to catch cording in stitches, and stitching toward short end of cord. Pivot, and stitch across tail, 1½" (1.3 cm) from end, centering cording.

12 Slide fabric onto short end of cord, turning tail right side out and encasing cording inside. Cut off cording close to stitched end.

13 Baste paws with pads 12" (30.5 cm) from upper edge of two leopard print chair sections. Follow steps 6 and 7 on pages 80 and 81, omitting topstitching. White section will be middle front, between sections that have paws. Baste lower paws to bottom, aligning inner edges to seam between white and print sections. Baste tail to center bottom of back middle section.

14 Finish chair, following steps 8 to 11 on page 81, omitting topstitching. When attaching bottom circle, stitch carefully across zipper teeth that extend into seam allowance, for chair made with long fur.

Diagram for the Side Pattern of the Beanbag Chair

Scale: one square on grid is equal to one square inch (2.5 cm2).

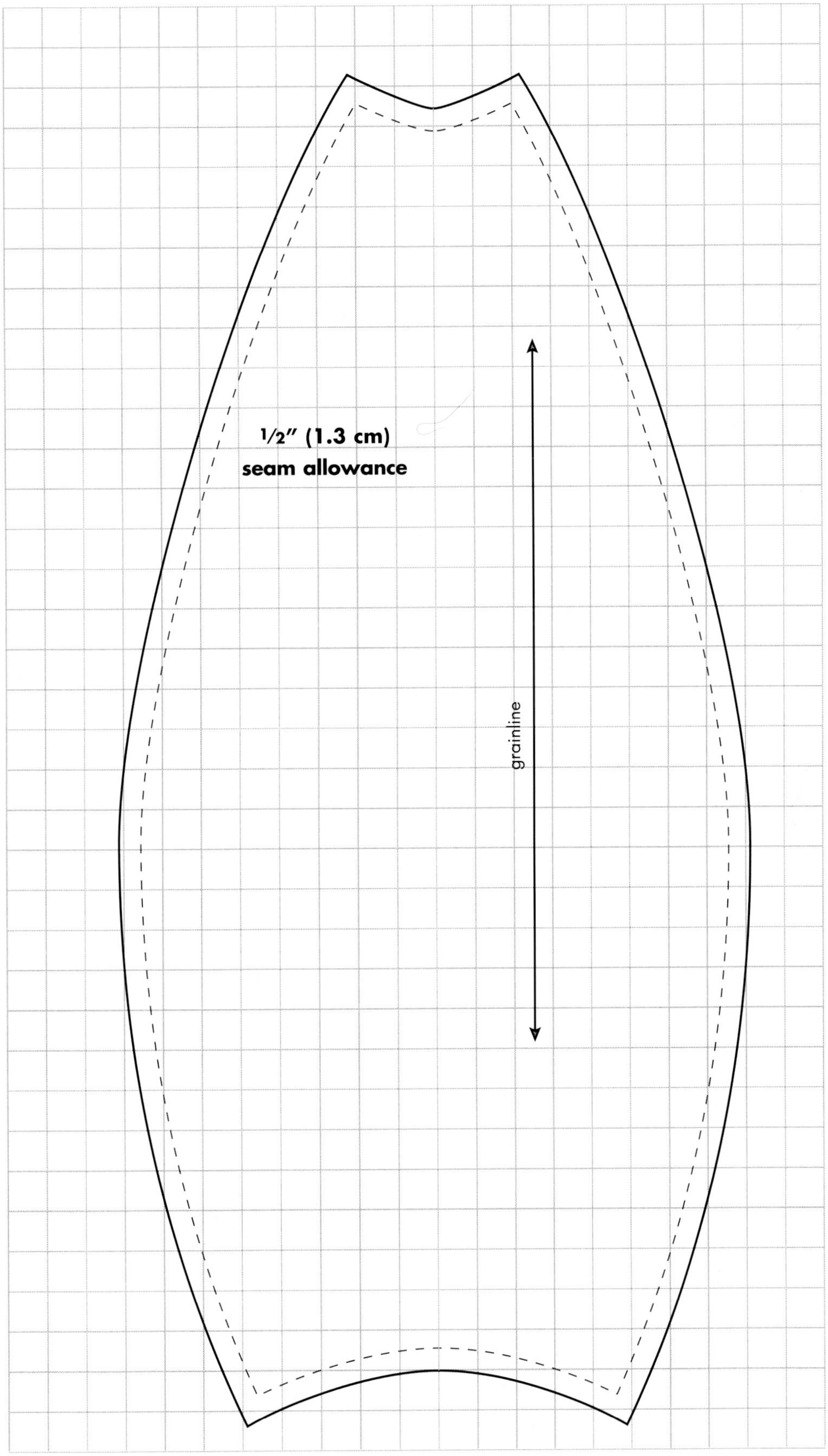

½" (1.3 cm) seam allowance

grainline

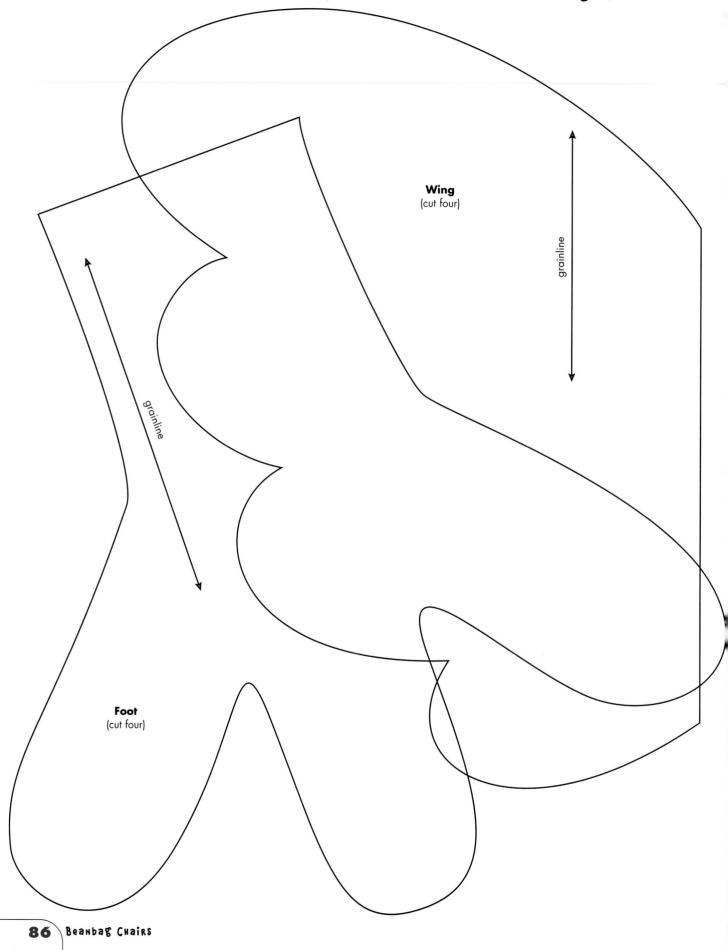

Wing
(cut four)

grainline

grainline

Foot
(cut four)

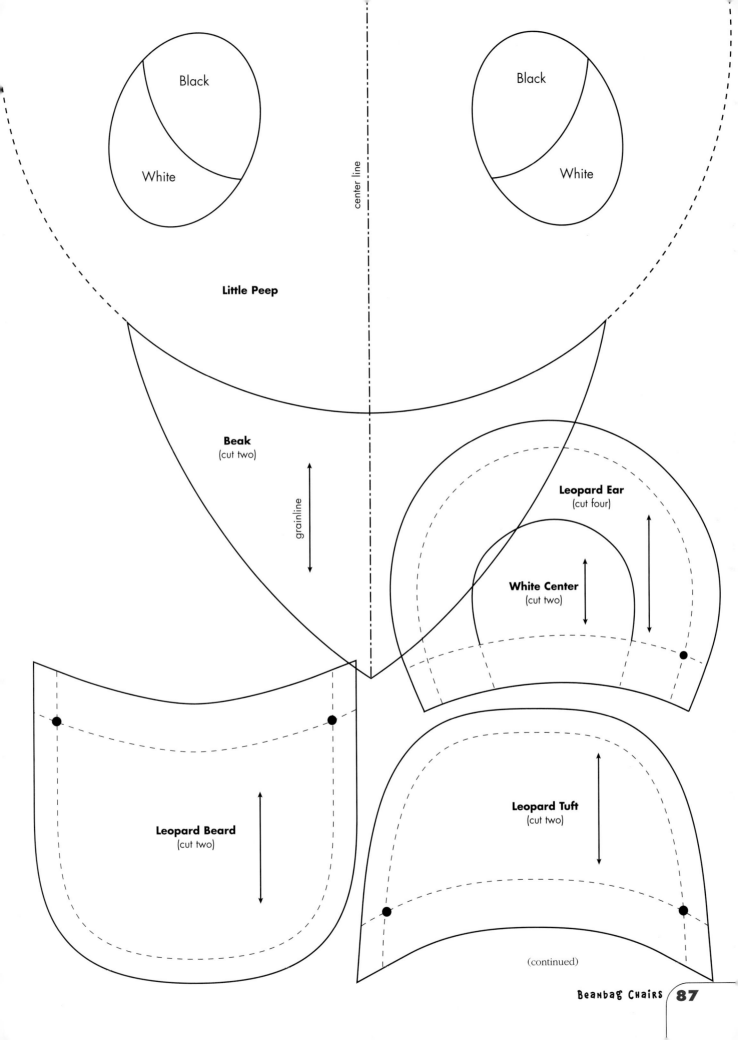

Black

White

Black

White

center line

Little Peep

Beak
(cut two)

grainline

Leopard Ear
(cut four)

White Center
(cut two)

Leopard Beard
(cut two)

Leopard Tuft
(cut two)

(continued)

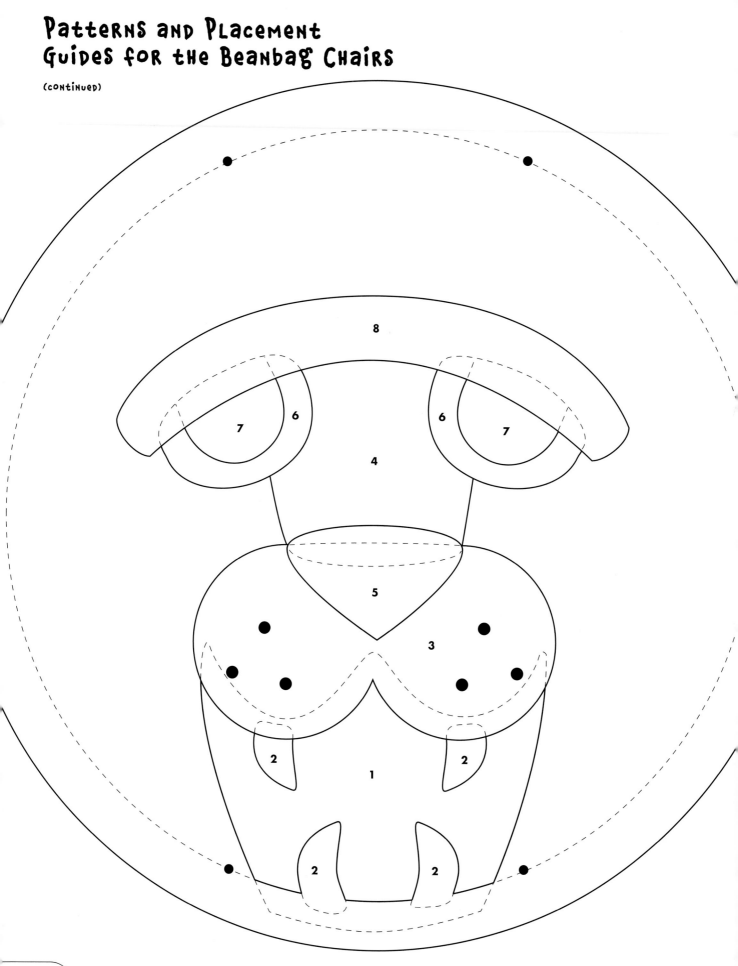

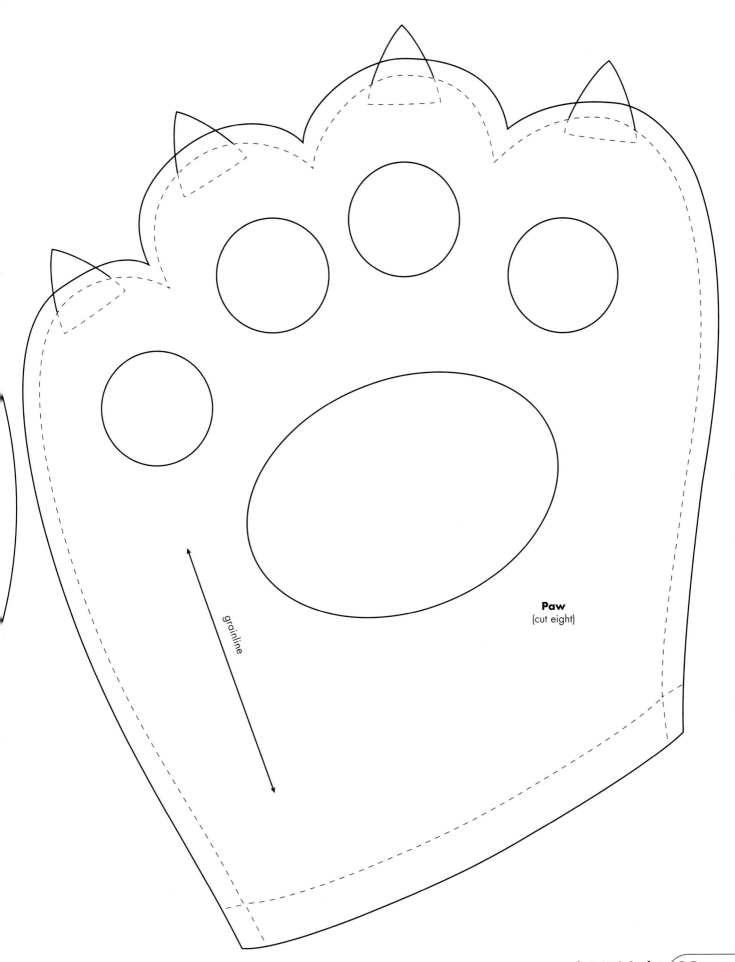

grainline

Paw
(cut eight)

FUN FLOAT

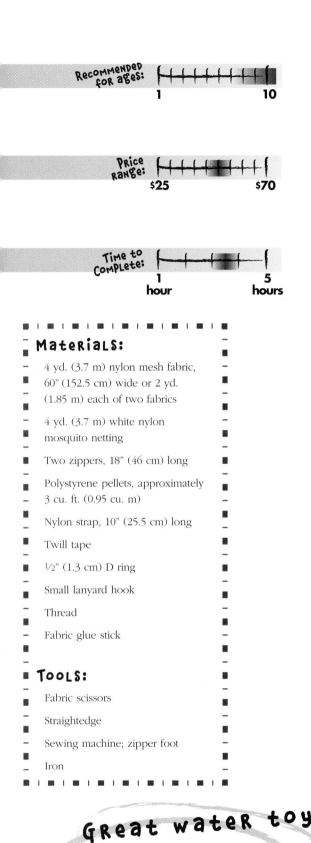

Recommended for ages:
1 — 10

Price Range:
$25 — $70

Time to Complete:
1 hour — 5 hours

MATERIALS:

- 4 yd. (3.7 m) nylon mesh fabric, 60" (152.5 cm) wide or 2 yd. (1.85 m) each of two fabrics
- 4 yd. (3.7 m) white nylon mosquito netting
- Two zippers, 18" (46 cm) long
- Polystyrene pellets, approximately 3 cu. ft. (0.95 cu. m)
- Nylon strap, 10" (25.5 cm) long
- Twill tape
- ½" (1.3 cm) D ring
- Small lanyard hook
- Thread
- Fabric glue stick

TOOLS:

- Fabric scissors
- Straightedge
- Sewing machine; zipper foot
- Iron

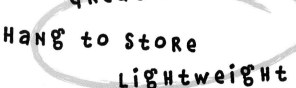

GReat wateR toy
HanG to StoRe
LiGHtweiGHt

Similar to the beanbag chairs on page 79, this version is great fun to play with in a swimming pool. The polystyrene pellets are naturally buoyant and the nylon mesh fabrics allow water and air in and out for comfortable floating and quick drying. A handy strap helps you remove it from the water and hang it to dry. A safety clasp prevents the inner zipper from opening and releasing pellets into the water.

By shifting the pellets around, the float can be molded into different shapes. One kid can mold it to his body and simply lounge in the water. Two kids can straddle it like a raft and motor it around with their hands or small paddles. The float might become home base for a lively game of water baseball. It even becomes a comfy deck chair during a swim break. Have no doubt, kids will make up lots of ways to play with it.

The float is intended for older kids who are able to swim and should always be used under adult supervision. It is not a lifesaving device. To prevent contamination by sand, algae, or little critters, avoid using the float at the beach.

1 Cut out the pieces as in steps 1 to 3 on page 80, using the pattern at right. Baste the side and top lining pieces to the underside of the outer pieces within the seam allowance. Melt the ends of the nylon strap to prevent fraying. Stitch the ends of the strap to opposite sides of top circle, on the right side.

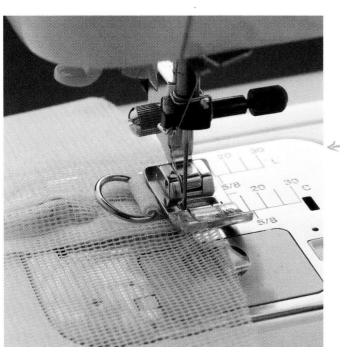

2 Follow steps 4 and 5, page 80, for the outer fabric and lining; on the lining, position the zipper with the lower stop ½" (1.3 cm) from the outer curve. Cut a 3" (7.5 cm) strip of twill tape; fold in half crosswise. Slip fold through D ring and fold in half again; baste to the bag bottom, at the top of the zipper seam.

3 Baste the bottom circles together, right sides up, slightly offsetting the zippers.

4 Complete the bag, following steps 6 to 10, pages 80 and 81. Pour polystyrene pellets into the bag; zip lining closed. Attach the lanyard hook to the zipper pull and lock onto the D ring to prevent the zipper from opening. Zip the outer opening closed.

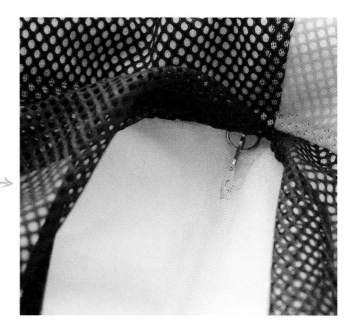

Diagram for the Side Pattern of Fun Float

Scale: one square on grid is equal to one square inch (2.5 cm²).

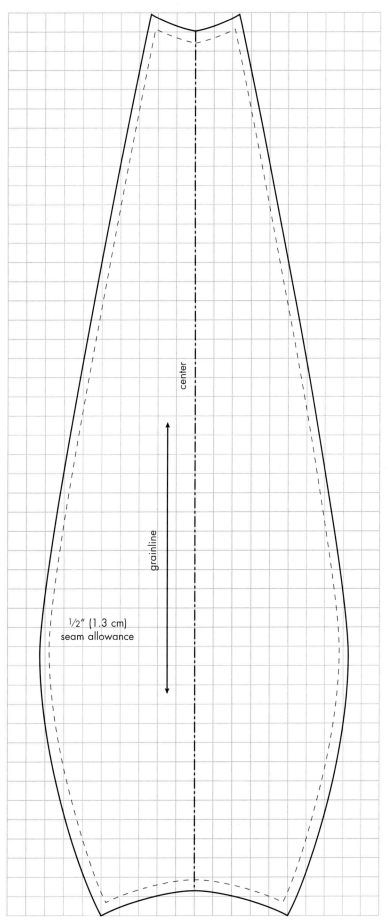

center

grainline

½" (1.3 cm) seam allowance

LEMONADE STAND

Recommended for ages: 1 — 10

Price range: $5 — $50

Time to Complete: 1 hour — 5 hours

Materials:

- Four 60" (152.5 cm) PVC pipes, 1" (2.5 cm) diameter
- Six elbows for 1" (2.5 cm) pipe
- Six tee fittings for 1" (2.5 cm) pipe
- Two rubber end caps to fit pipe
- Shelf with rounded corners, 12" × 36" × ¾" (30.5 × 91.5 × 2 cm)
- Four #8 × 1½" (3.8 cm) pan-head metal screws
- MDF board, ⅛" (3 mm) thick; chalkboard paint
- Velcro® straps
- Divided trays, no longer than 12" (30.5 cm)
- Plastic cap strips
- Small knobs
- Plastic sheeting for skirt, 60" × 20½" (152.5 × 52.3 cm), optional
- 60" (152.5 cm) self-adhesive hook and loop tape for attaching skirt, optional

Tools:

- Acetone and soft cloth; rubber gloves
- PVC pipe cutter or hack saw and sandpaper
- Drill and drill bits
- Clamps; rubber mallet
- Heavy duty glue; PVC cement

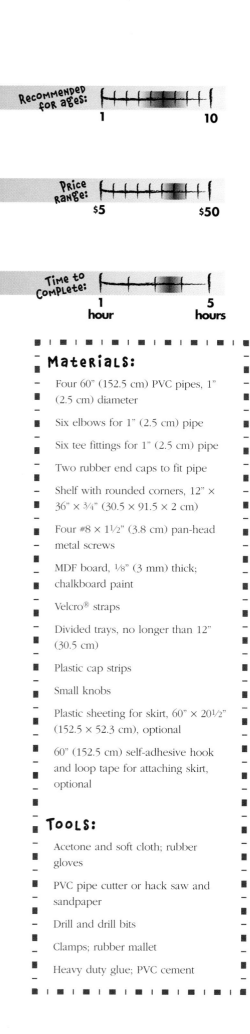

This nifty little concession stand is fun for outdoor or indoor play. It features a sturdy counter with handy drawers. A removable overhead signboard is painted with chalkboard paint on both sides so kids can advertise, list prices, and keep track of their profits.

A ready-made shelf is attached to the PVC pipe framework, keeping construction time to a minimum. Unlike the artist's easel on page 61, all of the joints in the lemonade stand are glued together for added stability. Sliding drawers are simply divided plastic trays with a lip along the sides. They are held in place with plastic cap strips, found in the molding department of the hardware store.

Sturdy but Light

Imaginative

Multipurpose

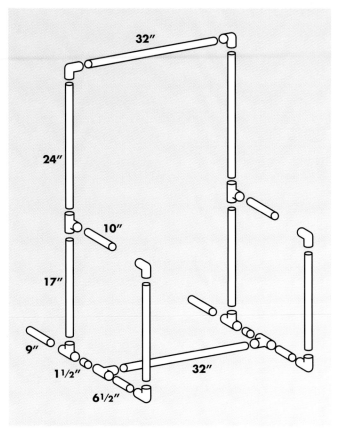

32"

24"

10"

17"

9"

1½"

6½"

32"

How to Make a Lemonade Stand

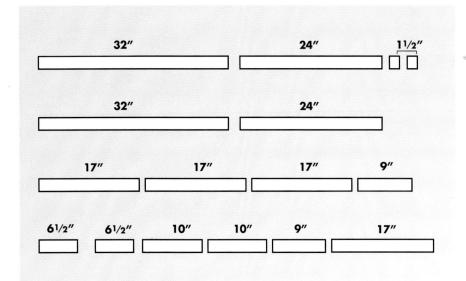

32"

24"

1½"

32"

24"

17"   17"   17"   9"

6½"   6½"   10"   10"   9"   17"

1 Clean pipes, using acetone and a soft cloth; wear rubber gloves. Carefully measure and mark these cut lengths for the pieces as indicated in the diagram: two 32" (81.5 cm), two 24" (61 cm), four 17" (43 cm), two 10" (25.5 cm), two 9" (23 cm), two 6½" (16.3 cm), and two 1½" (3.8 cm). Cut pieces, using PVC pipe cutter for a clean, even cut. Or use a hacksaw and sand the edges smooth.

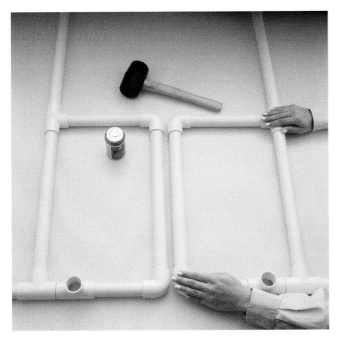

2 Assemble sides of stand. Glue in place, applying glue to inside of fittings; do not glue tee fittings for lower crossbar. Pound all joints together tightly, using rubber mallet. Place on a flat surface to check square alignment before glue sets.

3 Glue upper and lower crossbars in place; pound together securely. Attach end caps. Stand fame upright and check square alignment before glue sets.

4 Cut two lengths of cap strip the width of the shelf. On underside of shelf, position strips so that drawer fits snugly between them, at least 3" (7.5 cm) from shelf ends. Mark positions of cap strips. Remove drawer; glue cap strips in place. Repeat for any other drawers. Allow to dry. (continued)

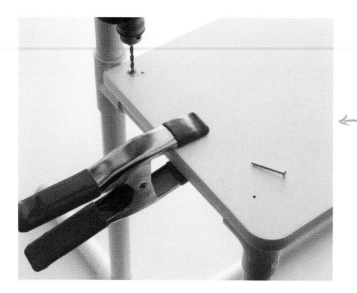

5 Center shelf on frame, with rounded corners forward and back edge against tee fittings. Clamp in place. Predrill screw holes through shelf and into fittings at four corners. Insert #8 × 1½" (3.8 cm) pan-head screws, securing shelf to frame. Remove clamps.

6 Cut MDF board to 9" × 31½" (23 × 80 cm). Using a ⅜" drill bit, drill holes ½" (1.3 cm) from the edges in the centers of the short ends and 8" (20.5 cm) from each end on one long edge.

7 Sand board lightly; wipe with tack cloth. Paint both sides of sign, using chalkboard paint; follow the manufacturer's directions.

8 Attach the signboard to the frame with removable Velcro® straps. Drill holes in the drawer ends; secure knobs to the drawer ends. Slide the drawers in place under the shelf.

Simply by changing the props and the chalkboard message, kids can use this versatile stand as a grocery store checkout lane, a theater box office, a bank teller's station, or a doctor's office check-in desk. It could become the teacher's desk when playing school or the toll booth for a parking ramp. Remove the chalkboard and hang a curtain from the upper support to use the stand for a puppet theater. For added drama, string mini lights across the front of the "stage" and up the side supports.

Use the divided-tray drawers for storing real or play money and a receipt book. Or, for playing "office," store pencils, paper clips, rubber bands, and notepads.

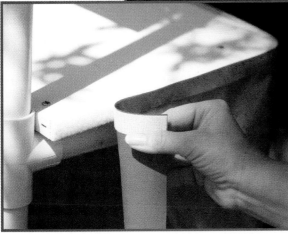

Fashion a simple, removable skirt for the front of the stand out of colorful plastic sheeting. Attach the skirt to the shelf edge with strips of self-adhesive hook and loop tape.

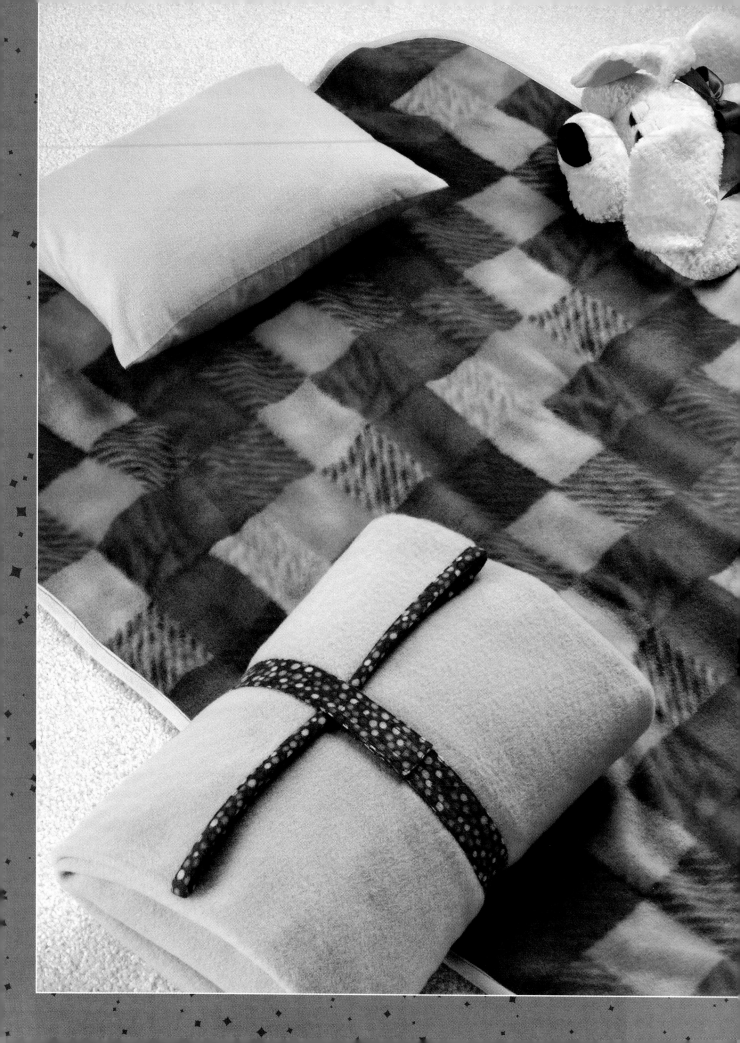

NAPTIME TOTE-ALONG

Recommended for ages:
1 — 10

Price range:
$5 — $50

Time to complete:
1 hour — 5 hours

Any time can be naptime with this handy blanket and pillow all rolled into one. Take it to daycare or preschool, Grandma's house or on a trip. When naptime rolls around, all a kid has to do is unroll it, cuddle up in it, and fall asleep. After a cozy doze, the blanket sides are simply folded in over the pillow, rolled up, and secured with a strap.

The blanket is made from snuggly, reversible polyester fleece, available in a rainbow of colors and oodles of prints. The attached pillow and matching binding are made from soft cotton flannel. Through a zipper closure, the pillow insert is easily removed for laundering the tote-along, assuming you can get it away from its owner!

MATERIALS:

- 1 yd. (0.95 m) polyester fleece or blanket-weight fabric, 60" (152.5 cm) wide
- 1¼ yd. (1.15 m) flannel
- Pillow form, 12" × 16" (30.5 × 40.5 cm)
- 2½" (6.5 cm) length of hook and loop tape, ¾" (2 cm) wide
- 9" (23 cm) zipper, in color to match flannel
- Glue stick
- Transparent tape, ½" (1.3 cm) wide

TOOLS:

- Sewing machine; zipper foot
- Fabric scissors
- Iron

Easy to wash
Easy to store
Soft & cuddly

How to Sew a Tote-along

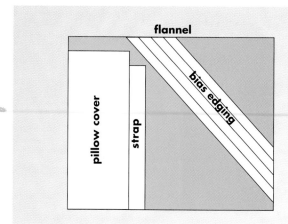

1. Cut a 36" × 45" (91.5 × 115 cm) rectangle of fleece for the blanket. Round the corners, using a saucer as a guide. Cut a 13" × 33" (33 × 84 cm) rectangle of flannel for the pillow cover. Cut a 3½" × 30" (9 × 76 cm) strip of flannel for the strap. Cut enough 2" (5 cm) bias strips of flannel to seam together to a length of 165" (419 cm); leave diagonal cuts at the ends.

2. Align the short ends of the pillow cover, right sides together; pin. Mark points 2" (5 cm) from each edge. Stitch ½" (1.3 cm) seam from edge to mark at each end, backstitching at marks. Machine-baste seam between marks. Press seam allowances open.

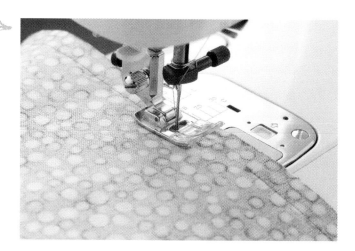

3. Apply glue stick lightly on face side of zipper. Place zipper face-down over basted section of seam, with zipper coil directly over seamline.

4. Mark top and bottom of zipper with pins on right side of fabric. Center 9" (23 cm) strip of ½" (1.3 cm) transparent tape over seamline. Using zipper foot, topstitch along one edge of tape, beginning at seam, pivoting at corners, and ending at seam on opposite end. Repeat for other side, stitching in same direction.

5. Pull threads to underside and knot at each end of zipper. Remove basting stitches over zipper.

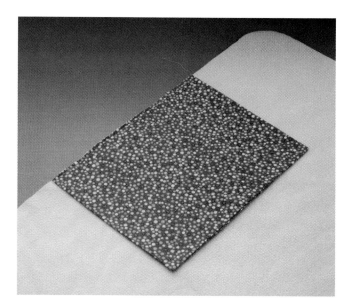

6. Fold pillow cover, right sides together, centering zipper. Stitch ½" (1.3 cm) seam on one long edge. Turn right side out; press. Pin open edges to center top of blanket fabric. Baste together ¼" (6 mm) from edges.

7 Fold strap in half lengthwise, right sides together. Stitch ¼" (6 mm) seam on one short end and long side. Turn right side out and press. Edgestitch on three finished sides of strap.

8 Stitch hook side of hook and loop tape to finished end of strap, ½" (1.3 cm) from end. Stitch loop side to opposite end, on opposite side, 1" (2.5 cm) from end. Baste unfinished end of strap to center bottom of blanket, with loop tape facing up.

9 Stitch bias strips together, using ¼" (6 mm) seams; press seam allowances open. Press under one long edge ⅜" (1 cm); press under ⅜" (1 cm) on the diagonal end where stitching will begin.

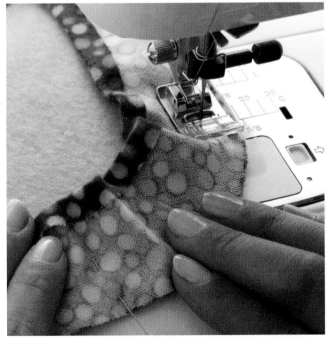

10 Stitch right side of bias strip to blanket back, matching raw edges and stitching ⅜" (1 cm) from edges. Begin on one long side. Ease strip around corners. Keep bias strip slightly taut on stretchy sides of blanket to avoid ripples. Overlap ends ½" (1.3 cm); trim excess diagonally.

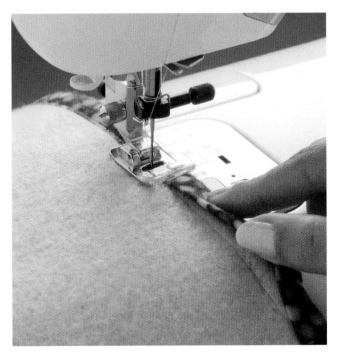

11 Turn bias to front. Align pressed fold to previous stitching line, encasing raw edges of pillow and strap; pin or secure with glue stick. Topstitch close to fold.

QUIET-TIME CUSHION

Recommended
for ages:

1   10

Price
range:

$25 $70

Time to
complete:

5   9
hours   hours

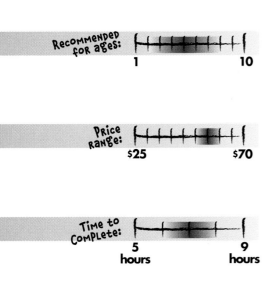

PERSONAL SPACE
WIPE-CLEAN
SURFACE

When it's time to cozy up to a good book, spend a little one-on-one time with a favorite toy, or watch cartoons, a quiet-time cushion gives a kid a place to get comfy. The bolster, attached to the floor cushion with Velcro®, invites a kid to lean back and relax. However, it is easily detached, so the cushion can be used alone for less quiet activities, such as tumbling and standing on one's head! The best fabric choice for this project is knit-back vinyl, also called "pleather," which is easy to sew, adheres to the Velcro well, and is also easy to wipe clean in case of spills. The foam bolster and high density foam for the mat are available at fabric stores and foam specialty stores.

Materials:

- Foam bolster, 36" (91.5 cm)
- High density foam, 2" (5 cm) thick, 36" × 40" (91.5 × 102 cm); piece together, if necessary, using foam glue
- 2 yd. (1.85 m) self-adhesive Velcro loop tape, 1½" (3.8 cm) wide
- 1 yd. (0.95 m) Velcro hook tape, 3" (7.5 cm) wide
- 2 yd. self-adhesive Velcro hook and loop tape, ¾" (2 cm) wide
- 3¾ yd. (3.45 m) knit-back vinyl fabric; thread to match
- Double-stick tape

Tools:

- Sewing machine; Teflon foot helpful when sewing vinyl
- Fabric scissors

1 Cut the cover 36½" (91.8 cm) wide with the length equal to the circumference of the bolster plus 3" (7.5 cm). Trace the bolster end on paper, and add ½" (1.3 cm) seam allowance all around; cut two mirror-image end pieces, using this pattern.

2 Center 35" (89 cm) strip of ¾" (2 cm) loop tape on one short end of main cover piece, with edge of tape ⅛" (3 mm) from raw edge; adhere or stitch. Turn fabric edge under 1" (2.5 cm); baste occasionally with double-stick tape. Stitch.

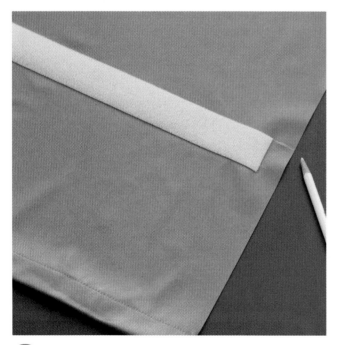

Hint: Test the self-adhesive Velcro® on a scrap of your fabric. If it does not hold securely, stitch along the outer edges of the Velcro to complete each step, using a medium length straight stitch.

3 Mark a line on right side of fabric the same distance from folded edge as length of bolster bottom (from front to back). Center 35" (89 cm) strip of 1½" (3.8 cm) loop tape next to line (between line and fold); adhere or stitch.

4 Turn under 1" (2.5 cm) on opposite end; stitch. On right side, center 35" (89 cm) strip of ¾" (2 cm) hook tape, ⅛" (3 mm) from fold; adhere or stitch.

Hint: Pin vinyl pieces together, keeping the pins within the seam allowances to avoid leaving pin holes in the fabric. Seam allowances can also be held together temporarily with double-stick tape.

5. Wrap fabric around bolster and fasten closure at back bottom. Mark all corners with 3⁄8" (1 cm) clip in seam allowance.

6. Remove cover; refasten closure. Baste closure edges together 3⁄8" (1 cm) from ends. Turn cover inside out.

7. Pin cover end piece to main piece, right sides together, matching slits to corners. Stitch 1⁄2" (1.3 cm) seam, pivoting at corners. Repeat for opposite end.

8. Turn cover right side out through closure. Insert bolster, pushing foam into corners; fasten closure.

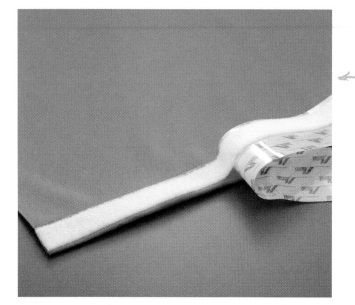

1. Cut fabric for the cushion bottom 36½" × 42" (91.8 × 107 cm). Cut fabric for the cushion top 40½" × 45½" (103 × 116 cm). Turn under 1" (2.5 cm) on one narrow end of cover bottom; stitch. On right side, center 35" (89 cm) strip of ¾" (2 cm) loop tape, ⅛" (3 mm) from fold; adhere or stitch.

2. Center a 35" (89 cm) strip of 1½" (3.8 cm) loop tape ¼" (6 mm) from the edge of the narrow tape; adhere or stitch.

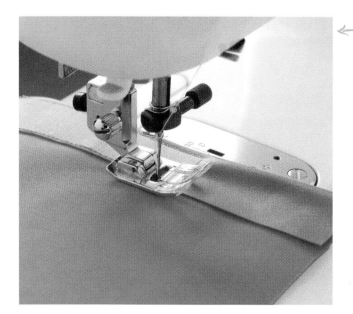

3. Center 35" (89 cm) strip of ¾" (2 cm) hook tape on one short end of cover top piece, with edge of tape ⅛" (3 mm) from raw edge; adhere. Turn fabric edge under 1" (2.5 cm) and stitch.

4. Mark 2½" (6.5 cm) corner darts in cover top at end opposite closure. Mark corner darts in closure end, 2½" (6.5 cm) from cut edge and 2" (5 cm) from finished edge.

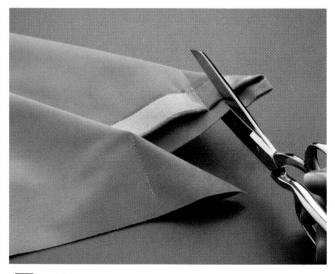

5. Fold corners diagonally, aligning marked lines; stitch, stopping ½" (1.3 cm) from raw edges on corners opposite closure. On closure corners, backstitch at finished edge. Trim excess fabric at corners to ½" (1.3 cm).

Hint: If you are unable to find pleather in the color you prefer, consider making the quiet-time cushion from cotton duck, sail cloth, or denim. The Velcro® would definitely have to be sewn on, so plan on buying the non-adhesive style. The covers can still be easily removed if laundering is necessary.

6 Pin top to bottom, right sides together, on three sides. At closure end, cover bottom extends 1" (2.5 cm) beyond top. Stitch ½" (1.3 cm) seam, pivoting at corners and backstitching to secure. Clip seam allowance of bottom to stitching at closure end.

7 Fasten closure at ends. Align remaining seam allowance of bottom to corner dart seam allowance; stitch over dart seamline.

8 Turn cover right side out. Insert cushion; fasten closure. To secure bolster to cushion end, fasten both pieces to 35" (89 cm) of plain hook tape, 3" (7.5 cm) wide.

HANDY DANDY BOOSTER SEAT

Recommended for ages: 1 — 10

Price range: $5 — $50

Time to Complete: 1 hour — 5 hours

MATERIALS:

- ⅝ yd. (0.6 m) fabric, 54" to 60" (137 to 152.5 cm) wide
- Fabric markers
- 9" (23 cm) sport zipper
- Thread
- Polyurethane foam, 13" (33 cm) square, 5" (12.7 cm) thick

TOOLS:

- Sewing machine; zipper foot
- Iron
- Fabric scissors
- Hand needle

For all the occasions when your little tyke needs a boost—dining out, going to the movies, lunch at the neighbor's house—sew up a personal cushy booster seat. The foam construction and handle make it lightweight and easy to carry. It even has a large zippered pocket for movie tickets, tissues, or towelettes.

Select mediumweight, tightly woven fabric that can be spot-cleaned when necessary, such as denim or sailcloth. Apply fabric-paint designs, handprints, or lettering to the fabric pieces before sewing them together.

ENCOURAGES independence

Convenient

1 Cut two 13½" (34.3 cm) squares of fabric for the top and bottom of the booster seat. Cut a 6" × 51" (15 × 129.5 cm) boxing strip for the sides. Cut two pocket pieces 3¼" × 10½" (8.2 × 26.7 cm). Cut a 5" × 8" (12.7 × 20.5 cm) strip for the handle.

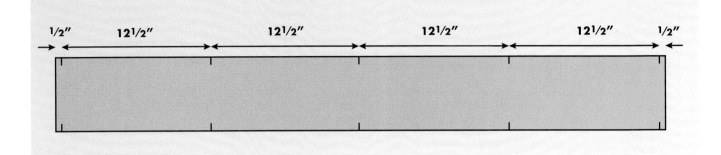

½"   12½"   12½"   12½"   12½"   ½"

2 Mark seamlines on both long sides of the boxing strip ½" (1.3 cm) from each end. Mark pivot points for corners 12½" (31.8 cm) apart, using ⅜" (1 cm) clips.

3 Center the zipper face-down on the right side of one long edge of a pocket piece, edges even. Stitch ⅛" (3 mm) from the zipper teeth, using a zipper foot. Repeat with the other pocket piece on the opposite side of the zipper.

4 Press seam allowances away from the zipper teeth. Topstitch on each side of the zipper ¼" (6 mm) from teeth.

5 Press under ½" (1.3 cm) on short ends of pocket. Pin pocket, right side up, in center of front section of boxing strip. Raw edges should align; trim excess pocket width, if necessary. Baste pocket to boxing strip ⅜" (1 cm) from raw edges. Topstitch short sides close to pressed folds.

6 Press handle in half lengthwise, wrong sides together; open. Turn in long edges to center fold; press. Fold in half, aligning outer folds. Topstitch close to outer folds on both sides.

7 Pin handle end to center of back boxing strip section 4" (10 cm) in from pivot point, with raw edges facing center. Stitch 1/8" (3 mm) from end. Repeat for other end of handle at other side of section.

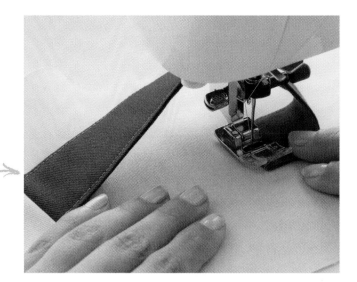

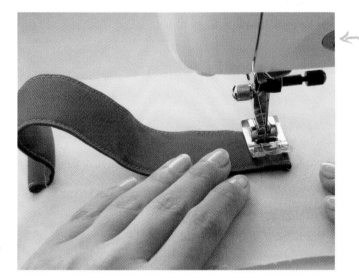

8 Turn handle in over raw edges; topstitch 3/8" (1 cm) from first stitching line to secure. Repeat for other end. Join short ends of boxing strip in 1/2" (1.3 cm) seam, forming ring; begin and end 1/2" (1.3 cm) from edges. Press open.

9 Mark pivot points on right side of top and bottom, 1/2" (1.3 cm) from corners. Press under 1/2" (1.3 cm) on back edge of bottom.

10 Pin boxing strip to top, matching pivot points. Stitch 1/2" (1.3 cm) seam, pivoting at corners; overlap stitches to secure.

11 Stitch boxing strip to bottom, leaving back side open; backstitch to secure. Turn cushion cover right side out.

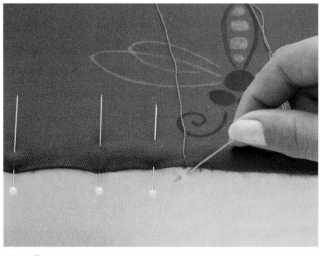

12 Compress foam and fold in half from front to back; insert into opening. Stretch cover to fit cushion smoothly. Pin opening closed; slipstitch.

BATH PONCHOS

Recommended for ages:

1   10

Price Range:

$5 $50

Time to Complete:

1 hour   5 hours

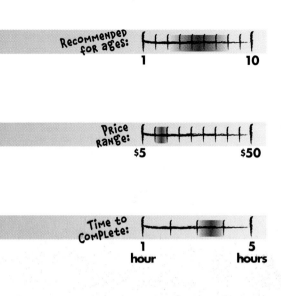

Squeaky-clean kids, fresh from the bathtub, can dry off and play a little make-believe in a soft, absorbent poncho. Made from two bath towels, the ponchos are styled to imitate some of nature's friendliest creatures. Create a perky puppy, a docile dolphin, or a lovable ladybug. You'll never have to play tug of war over bath time again.

Materials for Basic Poncho:

- Two bath towels
- ¼ yd. (0.25 m) contrasting fabric, such as plaid or animal-print cotton flannel or broadcloth, for ears and feet
- Scraps of black fabric for eyes and nose
- Paper-backed fusible web
- Tear-away stabilizer

Additional materials for dolphin:

- Scraps of black and white fabric for eyes
- Strip of black polar fleece
- Fusible poly fleece

Additional materials for ladybug:

- ¼ yd. (0.25 m) black polar fleece
- Small strip of red polar fleece
- ½ yd. (0.5 m) boning
- Small amount of polyester fiberfill
- Black single-fold bias tape or ½" (1.3 cm) grosgrain ribbon
- Glue stick

Tools:

- Fabric scissors
- Iron
- Sewing machine

Cuddly & absorbent
Fun to wear

How to Sew a Puppy Bath Poncho

1. Preshrink the bath towels. From one towel, cut a 10" × 22" (25.5 × 56 cm) rectangle for the hood, with one long edge along the selvage of the towel. From the same towel, cut two ear pieces and two foot pieces, using patterns on page 125. From contrasting fabric, cut two ear pieces and two foot pieces.

2. Fold hood piece in half along selvage. On the side opposite the selvage, use a saucer to round corner from fold to raw edges; trim.

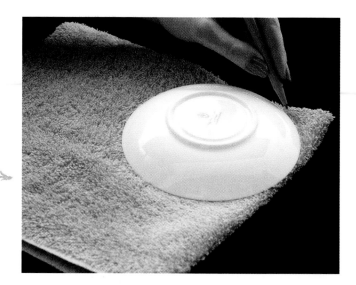

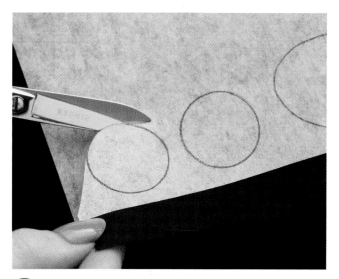

3. Fuse paper-backed fusible web to wrong side of black fabric; using patterns on page 121, trace eyes and nose onto paper side. Cut out pieces.

4. Remove the paper backing from the eyes and nose. Pin-mark center of hood at selvage. Following placement guide on page 121, fuse pieces to hood.

5. Set machine for satin stitching by adjusting zigzag stitch for closely spaced, wide stitches. Satin-stitch around eyes and nose, placing tear-away stabilizer under hood; satin-stitch the mouth as shown on the placement guide (page 121).

6. Place one ear piece from terry cloth and one from contrasting fabric right sides together. Stitch ¼" (6 mm) seam around curved edge, leaving the straight end unstitched; clip curves. Turn right side out. Repeat for remaining ear and both feet.

Hint: Bath ponchos are warm, absorbent, and full of fun from head to toes. They're also a great cover-up for the pool or beach. While you're out shopping, keep your eyes open for white sales and stock up on towels for future projects. Bath ponchos make great gifts, too!

7 Place one ear, contrasting side down, with straight end on placement line and with ear lying above face. Stitch in place along the open end, using wide, short zigzag stitches. Repeat for other ear.

8 Fold the hood in half, with right sides together, matching raw edges. Stitch ⅜" (1 cm) center back seam on the curved side of the hood; finish seam, using zigzag or overlock stitch.

9 Fold remaining bath towel in half, with lower edge of top layer 1" (2.5 cm) above lower edge of bottom layer. Mark the center of the fold; on fold, measure and mark 5¼" (13.2 cm) on each side of center.

10 Unfold the bath towel. Slash the towel between the end markings, for a 10½" (26.7 cm) opening. (continued)

11 Pin the hood to the towel at opening, right sides together; match the center back seam of the hood to center marking on longer side of towel. Front edges of hood will not meet.

12 Stitch hood to body in ⅜" (1 cm) seam. Zigzag or overlock seam allowances together, continuing across the slash between edges of hood in front.

13 Fold seam allowances toward the body. Topstitch through all layers, ¼" (6 mm) from the seamline; continue stitching across the front opening.

14 Pin feet, contrasting sides down, to wrong side of towel front, at lower edge and 6" (15 cm) from sides; overlap edges ½" (1.3 cm).

15 Stitch, using short, wide zigzag stitches. Topstitch through all layers, ¼" (6 mm) from the lower edge of the towel.

Hint: Bath towels come in a range of sizes. Select smaller towels for younger children. If the hood seems too large for a small child, stitch a dart across the seam near the back curve.

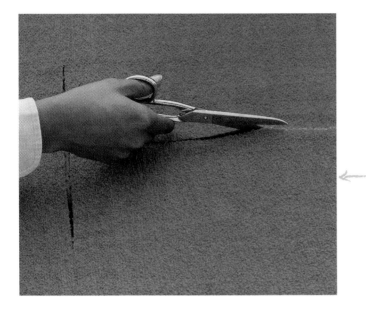

1 Cut and prepare the hood as in steps 1 and 2, page 116. Cut the fins, tail, and nose from the remaining towel fabric, using the patterns on pages 122, 124, and 125. Follow step 3 for black and white circles for eyes; fuse black circles to white circles, and satin stitch inner curve. Apply eyes as in steps 4 and 5, following placement guide on page 122. Stitch hood as in step 8, page 117.

2 Follow steps 9 and 10, placing marks 5½" (14 cm) from center for an 11" (28 cm) opening. Cut a 13½" (34.3 cm) slit down the center back.

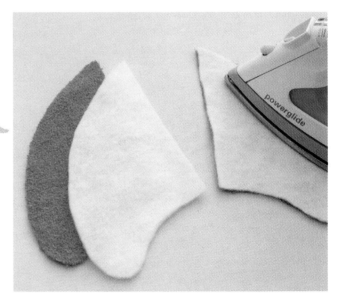

3 Cut two pieces of poly fleece, using the back fin pattern. Fuse the fleece to the wrong side of each fin. Place fins right sides together; stitch, leaving straight edge open. Turn right side out.

4 Baste back fin to one side of back slit, right sides together, with top of fin 6½" (16.3 cm) from upper edge.

5 Place back slit edges right sides together; stitch ¼" (6 mm) seam, tapering to a point at the bottom. Zigzag or overlock raw edges together. Attach hood, following steps 11 to 13, opposite.

6 Prepare side fins, nose, and tail as in step 6, page 116, using terry cloth for both sides. Cut narrow strips of black polar fleece for mouth line; stitch in place through center of strip. Stitch fins to center sides of poncho front; stitch tail to center bottom of back as in steps 14 and 15, opposite.

How to Sew a Ladybug Bath Poncho

1 From a black towel, cut and prepare the hood as in steps 1 and 2, page 116. Cut twelve terry cloth feet, page 124. Cut eight polar fleece spots and four antennae, page 123. Follow steps 3 and 4 for applying eyes, following placement guide on page 123. Cut ¼" × 2½" (6 mm × 6.5 cm) strip of red polar fleece for mouth; stitch in place through center of strip. Make two buttonholes in hood at marks. Stitch hood as in step 8, page 117.

2 Place two antennae right sides together; stitch on seamline to dots, backstitching to secure. Trim seams and clip corners. Turn right side out. Stuff round end firmly with fiberfill, using pencil eraser.

3 Repeat step two for second antenna. Insert antennae through buttonholes. Spread open ends apart and stitch to inside of hood.

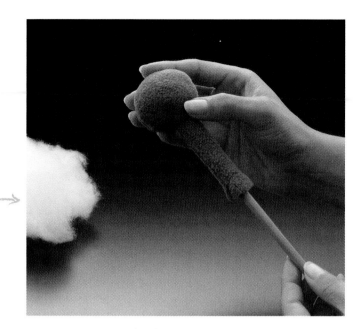

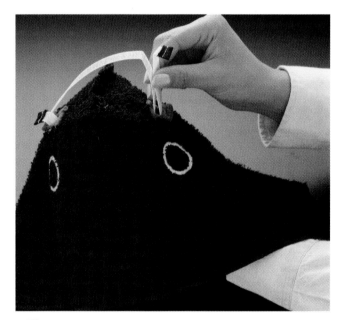

4 Cut 17½" (44.3 cm) of boning; bind ends with small strips of bias tape. Crease boning sharply ½" (1.3 cm) from end. Crease in opposite direction 3" (7.5 cm) from first crease, and again 3" (7.5 cm) from second crease. Repeat at opposite end. Insert double 3" (7.5 cm) extensions up into antenna stems.

5 Stitch short ends of boning to hood; tack boning to hood between antennae. Cut a 1½" × 7½" (3.8 × 19.3 cm) strip of black polar fleece. (Gray was used for clarity.) Glue-baste over exposed boning; stitch around edges.

6 Prepare poncho body as in steps 9 and 10, page 117. Glue-baste bias tape or ribbon down center of back; fold under lower end ⅜" (1 cm). Stitch close to both edges and across bottom to secure.

7 Glue-baste spots in place as desired; edgestitch. Make six feet as in step 6, page 116. Stitch to front sides of poncho as in steps 14 and 15. Attach hood, following steps 11 to 13.

Patterns and Placement Guides for the Ponchos

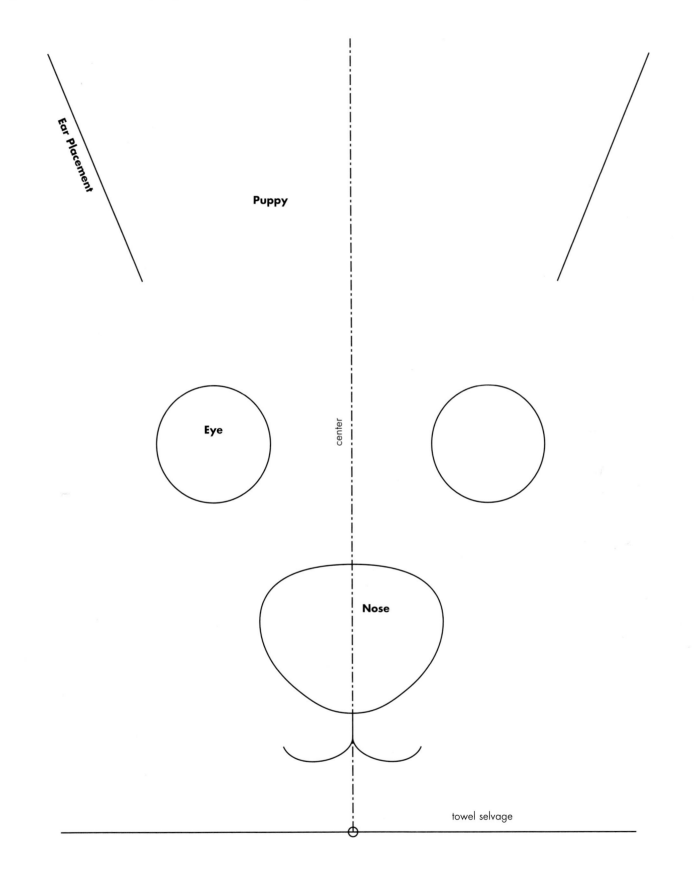

Ear Placement

Puppy

center

Eye

Nose

towel selvage

(continued)

Patterns and Placement Guides for the Ponchos
(CONTINUED)

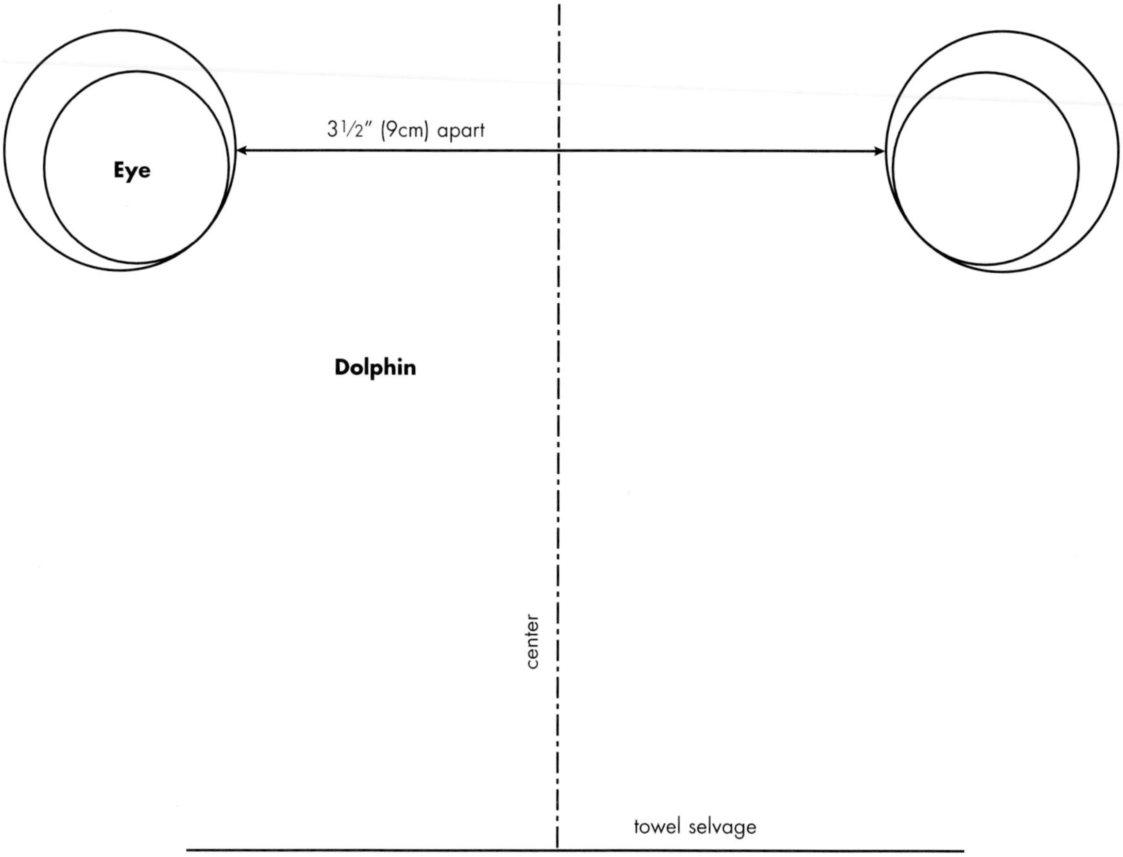

Eye

3½" (9cm) apart

Dolphin

center

towel selvage

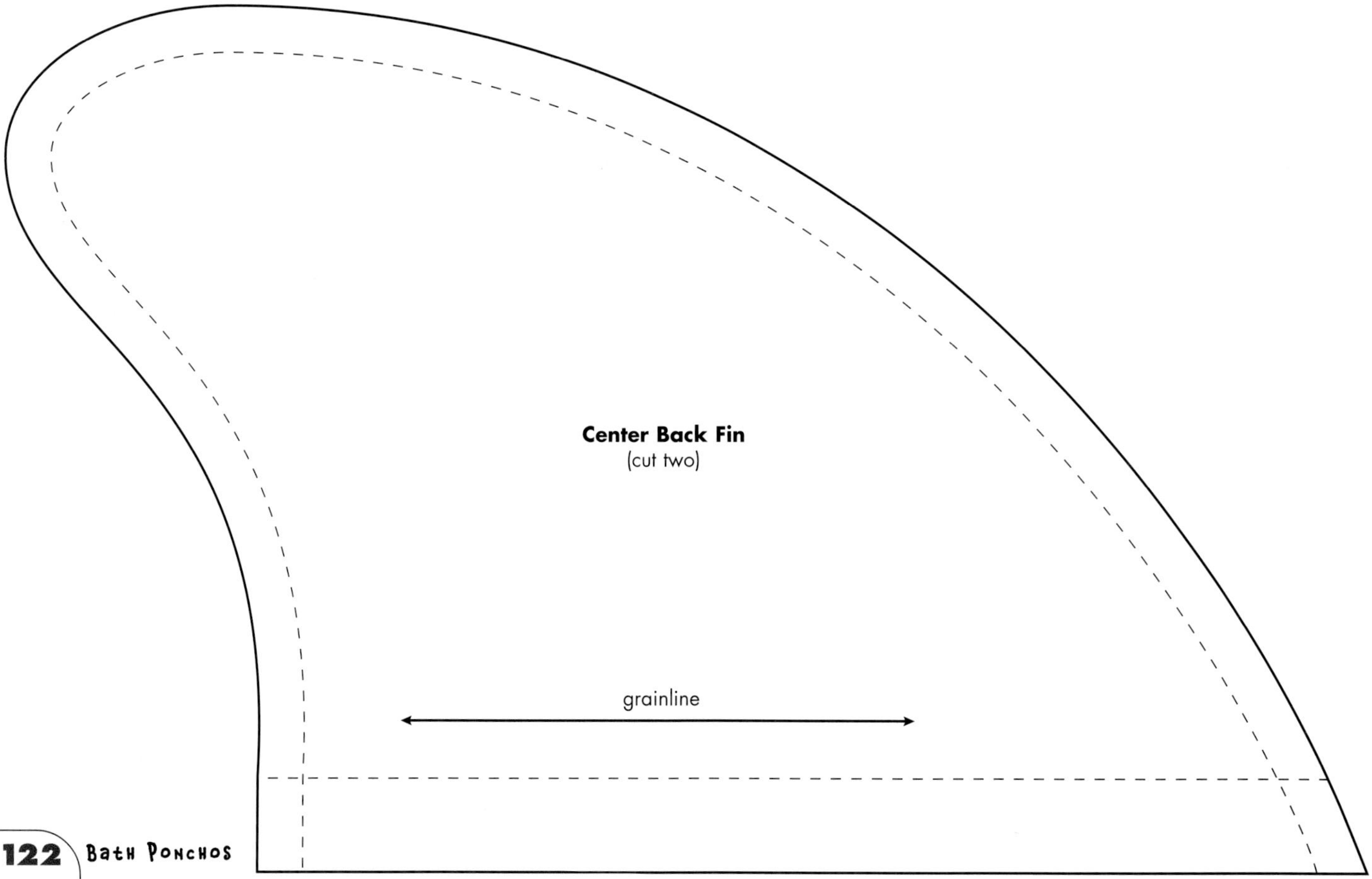

Center Back Fin
(cut two)

grainline

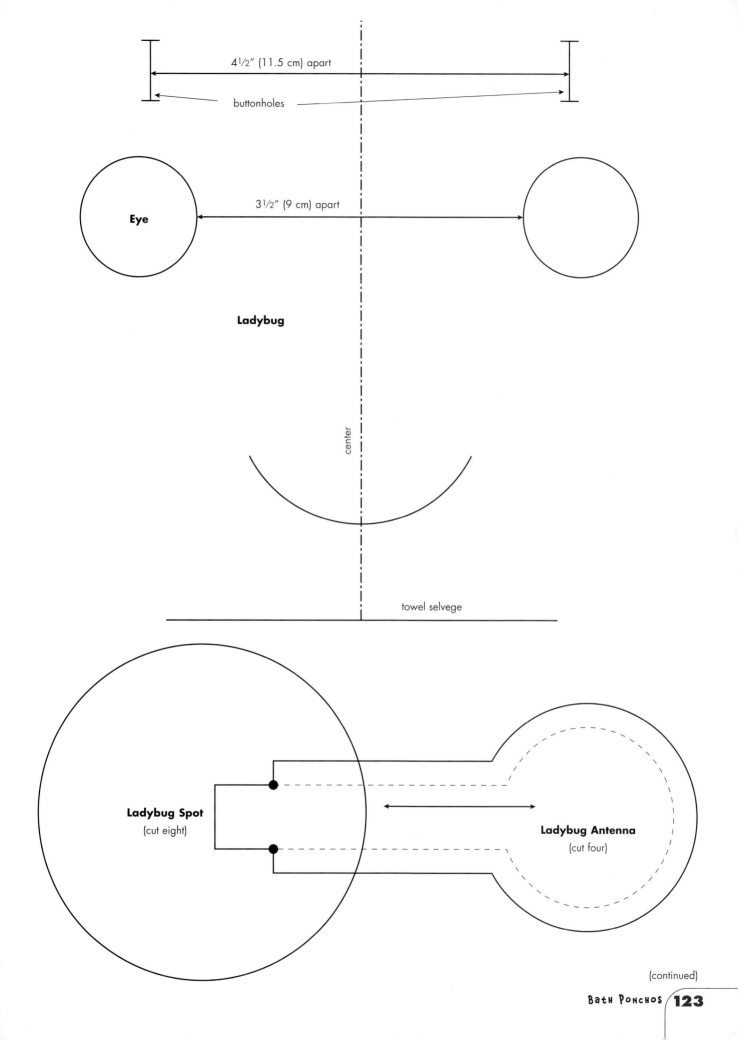

4¹⁄₂" (11.5 cm) apart

buttonholes

Eye

3¹⁄₂" (9 cm) apart

Ladybug

center

towel selvege

Ladybug Spot
(cut eight)

Ladybug Antenna
(cut four)

(continued)

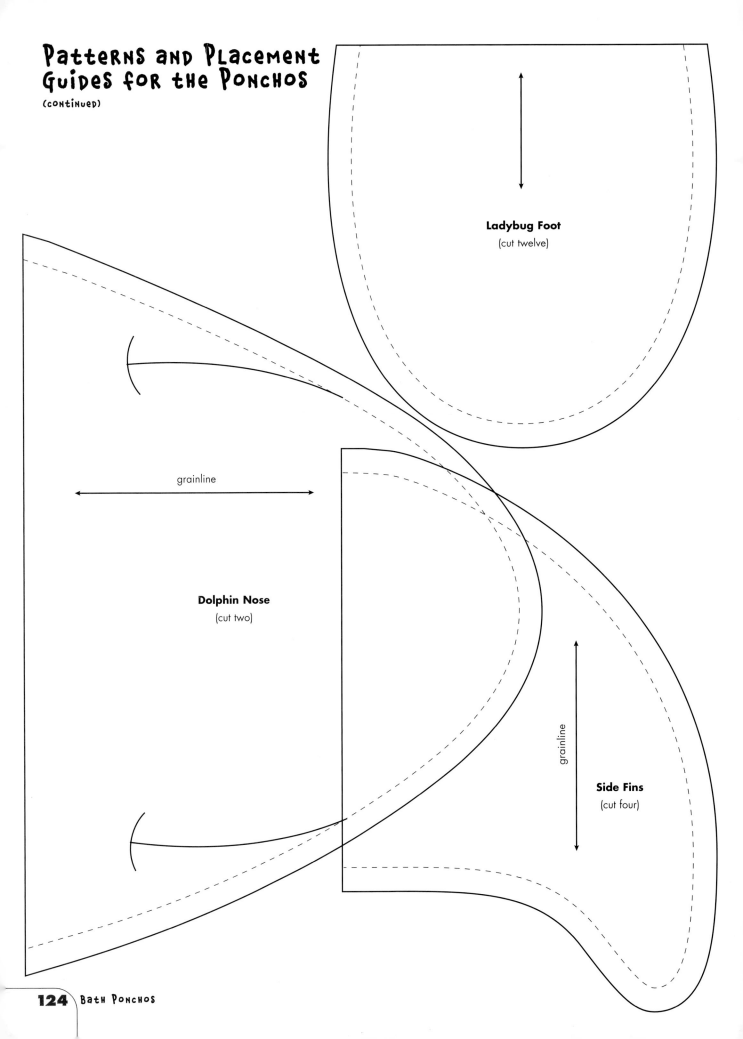

Ladybug Foot
(cut twelve)

grainline

Dolphin Nose
(cut two)

grainline

Side Fins
(cut four)

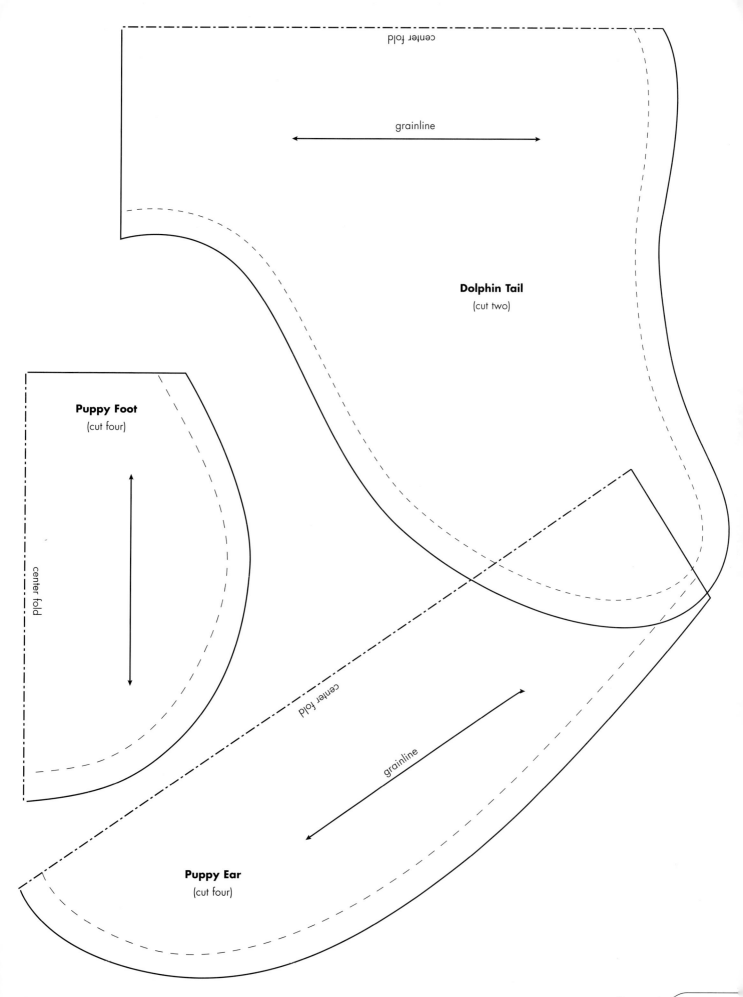

center fold

grainline

Dolphin Tail
(cut two)

Puppy Foot
(cut four)

center fold

center fold

grainline

Puppy Ear
(cut four)

Index